Dictation

New methods, new possibilities

Paul Davis and Mario Rinvolucri

CAMBRIDGE
UNIVERSITY PRESS

To Caleb Gattegno
absent from the bibliographies but vividly present in the
minds of many practitioners.

Dictation was originally published in pilot form by Pilgrims Publications,
Canterbury, England. This Cambridge University Press edition has been
reorganised and revised.

Published by the Press Syndicate of the University of Cambridge
The Pitt Building, Trumpington Street, Cambridge CB2 1RP
40 West 20th Street, New York, NY 10011-4211 USA
10 Stamford Road, Oakleigh, Melbourne 3166, Australia

© Cambridge University Press 1988

First published 1988
Seventh printing 1995

Printed and bound in Great Britain
by Athenæum Press Ltd, Gateshead, Tyne & Wear

Library of Congress catalogue card and number: 87–30010

British Library cataloguing in publication data

Davis, Paul
Dictation: new methods, new possibilities
(Cambridge handbooks for language teachers).
1. Dictation (Educational Methods).
2. Language and languages – Study
and teaching
I. Title   II. Rinvolucri, Mario
407   P53

ISBN 0 521 34299 6 hard covers
ISBN 0 521 34819 6 paperback

GO

Contents

Acknowledgements

We would like to thank the staff and students of the Cambridge Eurocentre who helped to test these materials. In particular classes B5, Winter 1985, and Y3, Autumn 1985.

Many ideas have been developed and improved in teacher training workshops. In this context there are many colleagues and sub-groups to be thanked. We found the reaction of a group of Pitman teachers in London particularly formative.

We would like to thank John Morgan for reacting to this material primarily as a teacher. Other Pilgrims colleagues and students have helped a lot.

Thanks to Michèle Debackère.

The authors and publishers are grateful to the authors, publishers and others who have given permission for the use of copyright material identified in the text. It has not been possible to identify or locate the sources of all the material used and in such cases the publishers would welcome information from copyright owners.

Jan H. Brunwand and W. W. Norton for the extract on p. 12; Times Newspapers Ltd for the article on p. 41; Alex Brummer and Michael White for the article on p. 42; New Scientist for the visual problem on p. 56; Tony Parker and Heinemann Educational Books for the extract on p. 61; Peace Pledge Union for the extract from their leaflet on p. 63.

Introduction

What is dictation?

Some of you may remember dictation from your schooldays with pleasure, some may have felt it boring, while some may have found it an encouraging exercise. In many cases the teacher probably read you the text, dictated it, and then read it a third time so you could check through. To many people this, and nothing else, *is* dictation.

The picture begins to change if you ask yourself a series of questions:

Who gives the dictation, and who to?
Who controls the pace of the dictation?
Who chooses or creates the text?
Who corrects it?

If all power remains in the hands of the teacher, then we have a bleak, traditional landscape. But dictation can be otherwise.

Sometimes, when introducing teacher training techniques in teacher training workshops, we have asked 'How many of you do dictation in your classes?' At first only a few hands go up. There is inhibition in the air – can one admit to doing something as reprehensible and old-fashioned as dictation in what is meant to be a progressive, 'communicative' workshop? What might colleagues think? But if we repeat the question more hands go up. It normally turns out that in any average group of European teachers more than half *do* use dictation either regularly or from time to time in their teaching. And with good reason.

A new methodology for an age-old exercise

This book is an attempt to put a useful but now undervalued area of work back on the language-teaching map, and to endow it with a methodology that makes it attractive to a broad range of teachers and students within current approaches to language learning and teaching.

To brainstorm a new methodology for dictation we asked ourselves a number of basic questions. The full answers to these questions constitute the body of this book. What follows is a peep at some questions and answers.

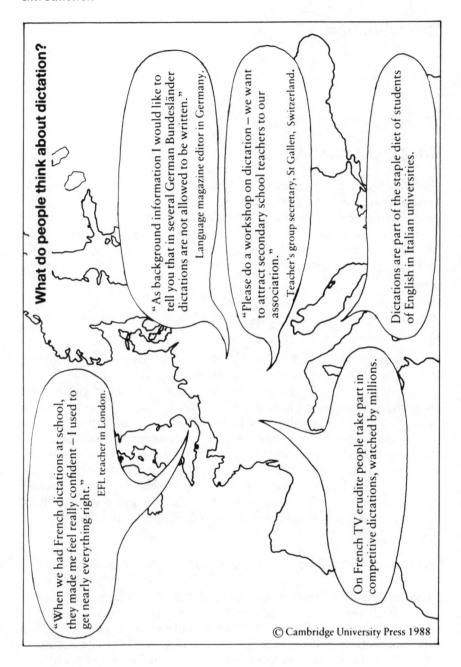

What do people think about dictation?

"When we had French dictations at school, they made me feel really confident – I used to get nearly everything right."

EFL teacher in London.

"As background information I would like to tell you that in several German Bundesländer dictations are not allowed to be written."

Language magazine editor in Germany.

"Please do a workshop on dictation – we want to attract secondary school teachers to our association."

Teacher's group secretary, St Gallen, Switzerland.

Dictations are part of the staple diet of students of English in Italian universities.

On French TV erudite people take part in competitive dictations, watched by millions.

© Cambridge University Press 1988

Who dictates?

- the teacher
- three voices on a tape; the student chooses the one she wants to take dictation from
- two students dictate to each other
- in the language lab the student takes dictation from her own voice on her own tape

Who chooses the texts?

- the coursebook writer
- the teacher
- the students
- the teacher offers several texts and the students choose
- the students offer texts and the teacher chooses

How long should the text be?

- a single word
- a sense group
- a whole passage
- a passage read in a continuous loop

How should the voice dictating sound?

- a whisper
- a shout
- the voice dictating is speaking, not reading
- the voice sings
- the voice reads to a background of music
- the person dictating has just done a relaxation exercise (and so have those listening)

Must the listener write down everything?

- yes, the whole text
- yes, the whole text plus the listener's own reaction
- no, selected bits of the text
- no, only the parts of the text the listener agrees with
- no, change the text to what the listener wants it to say

⟫→

Introduction

Who corrects the dictation?

- the student corrects herself
- the student corrects another listener's script
- the computer corrects
- the teacher corrects
- nobody does

Why use dictation?

Ten good reasons:

The students are active during the exercise

This apparently obvious point first came home to us forcefully when one of us started learning German at our local evening institute. To begin with, the teacher was talking 90 per cent of the time and never used pair or group work. The average student in a group of 15 people produced no more than eight or ten utterances in a 90 minute session. And the group met only once a week. Not much activity there. Then the teacher began to give the group dictations. This was marvellous for the students because they could be actively engaged in producing German on the page while the teacher retained full 'magisterial' control of the group. Suddenly, in this old-fashioned exercise, the student was allowed to become a *subject* again, instead of being only the *object* of the teacher's language flood. The students became subjects in the sense that they were actively engaged in creating visual German across the page in front of them.

Dictation is one of those exercises in which, if it is well done, the teacher's planned activity prompts reactions, simultaneously and immediately subsequently, by *all* the students in the group.

The students are active after the exercise

There is no call for the teacher to take on responsibility for correcting dictation scripts. Such work requires care, of course, but it does not require the kind of linguistic judgement that only the teacher can make. Correcting a dictation is a straightforward task which students are quite capable of doing for themselves, extending their activity from the dictation into the correction phase and providing them with opportunities to 'over-learn' the language as well as to collaborate with each other in the learning process. Such work is a good introduction to the habit of student self-correction, and in particular collaborative correction.

approaches. The teacher can usefully introduce these in more difficult areas, such as working on written compositions.

Dictation leads to oral communicative activities

Many of the exercises in this book show how dictation can be used as a lead-in to thoughtful communication by and between students. For example, the teacher can decide to dictate an interactive text – one in which the students not only write down what they hear but also react to it in writing. An example* would be a set of simple questions to set down and answer: 'If I came to your home as a guest //[†] what would you show me first? // what would you offer me to eat? // where would you let me sleep?' etc. Following the dictation, the students work in small groups comparing their answers; the 'inside self' thinking that has taken place during the dictation phase leads naturally into comparing experiences with other members of the group.

Dictation fosters unconscious thinking

With intermediate and advanced groups – any group in fact where it is possible to select a text that the students find quite easy to simply reproduce – dictation tends to occupy only a part of the students' minds. But important things can be brewing underneath, triggered by the language of the dictation. Perhaps an example is needed:

In *Once Upon a Time*, John Morgan offers an exercise in which he reads these words to the group at very high speed:

village
emigrate
marriage
absence
pregnant
shame
attack
destruction
birth
deep well
suicide

---

* This exercise was created in a brainstorming session by a group of colleagues at the Brighton IATEFL convention in 1985.
† The double oblique // is used in this book to mark pauses in dictation.

Introduction

The students invariably groan and grumble because none of them has managed to catch all the words. They are asked to pool what they have managed to get down, and so between them recreate the full list. The teacher then asks them to write down the story that the words imply.

What is important here is that the dictation phase – taking down the words – is simply the incubation phase for the story-making. On the surface of it the students are working on the reconstruction of the list, and complaining about the teacher's unreasonable behaviour as they do so. But all the time their minds are unconsciously working around the implications of the words in the set, building up a powerful base for the story creation. Two tasks are in motion at the same time at different mental levels. Dictation is ideal for occupying the conscious mind while stimulating the unconscious into action.

Dictation copes with mixed-ability groups

Here is a familiar problem: an Italian teacher faces a first-year group of 15-year-olds who have just come up from middle school. The majority of them have done three years of English (with varying results), but a minority studied French in middle school and are virtual beginners in English. In this extreme instance of a mixed-ability group, dictation remains a feasible exercise; indeed, properly conducted, it can capitalise on the range of abilities.

For example, the teacher chooses a text which is relatively easy for the most advanced students. She asks these students to do the dictation with no help at all. To the beginners, on the other hand, she gives out the text with only 10 to 15 words left out. Their task, while the others are writing away continuously, is to listen carefully, to try to understand the whole, and to fill in their missing words. At the end of the dictation, the more advanced students explain the text to the beginners and check the words they have inserted. The level of the text used, and the number of gaps left, can be varied to meet particular needs. Many dictation exercises help the teacher not only to cope with, but also to actually exploit positively, the range of abilities in the group.

Dictation deals with large groups

A teacher can give a dictation to a student one-to-one; yet, unlike most techniques, dictation is equally feasible with groups of 20 or 60 or 200, and there are plenty of groups of this size around the world. Indeed, dictation is one of the few approaches to teaching and learning in the large group context that has a reasonable chance of engaging the students in active language use. If the teacher does use dictation with large groups, she needs to be specially sure that her voice is capable of reaching all of the students clearly and expressively (see 'Tips for reading aloud' on page 9).

Dictation will often calm groups

If the teacher is working with a group with discipline problems, or simply one that is feeling skittish, it is useful to have an exercise which calms everyone down. In dictation, apart from the implicit control of topic and activity and pace, there is often a rhythmical, semi-hypnotic aspect to the exercise that puts everybody, including the teacher, into a slight trance (see Bandler & Grinder, 1981).

Dictation is safe for the non-native teacher

Recent trends in methodology have encouraged many exercises that are very open-ended; they depend heavily for their full success on the teacher's command of the target language, and thus impose a heavy burden on the teacher. This is all very well for the native speaker, but many teachers, through no fault of their own, have not achieved a level of English – accuracy of grammar, breadth of vocabulary, or sensitivity to stylistic variation, for example – that leaves them feeling comfortable with such exercises. Dictation, however, is something that teachers can prepare fully in advance. The language it generates is known; it is not an exercise that will take teachers by surprise in the class by exposing them to unexpected language.

For English, it is a technically useful exercise

Decoding the sounds of this particular language and recoding them in writing is a major learning task. In teaching other languages to non-native speakers, Spanish, for example, dictation is relatively less useful because the relationship between the sound system and the spelling is not especially problematic. Think, however, of what can face the learner of English. For example:

I went to *Slough*.   (rhymes with *cow*, not *off*)
She has a bad *cough*.   (rhymes with *off*, not *cuff*)
You're looking *rough*.   (rhymes with *cuff*, not *too*)
It's coming *through*.   (rhymes with *too*, not *four*)
That's what I *thought*.   (rhymes with *four*)

This kind of complexity – the regularities of sound/spelling as well as the oddities – in itself amply justifies dictation as an exercise.

For a divergent nineteenth-century view see page 122.

Dictation gives access to interesting text

Most teachers come across bits of text which interest them and would be of interest to their students – newspaper articles, magazines, bits of books, even bits of textbooks. Often such texts have a topicality or curiosity that will attract students in spite of potential linguistic difficulties. The teacher who has a range of dictation strategies at her disposal will be able to exploit these texts as they arise, employing techniques that will increase or decrease the difficulty of the text to match the needs and abilities of the group. And students will respond to the effort and opportunism of their teacher – perhaps adding their own. finds to the collection.

How to find your way around this book

The contents list shows you the sequence of sections and exercises.

The introduction to each section sets out the special features of the exercises in each section. A good way of skimming through the book is to hop from one of these introductions to the next.

The exercises give detailed explanations for the teacher, and usually include a sample text. In addition, each exercise carries a diagram showing the level for which the sample text is particularly appropriate, and the levels at which, with modification, the activity can be useful, like this:

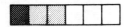

This box appears at the beginning of every exercise to show the general level of the exercise. The different levels are:

> Beginner/Elementary
> Lower intermediate
> Mid-intermediate
> Upper intermediate
> Advanced
> Proficiency

with Beginner/Elementary on the left, and Proficiency on the right. The example above is from an exercise presented here for beginners, but the teacher can easily adapt it for lower and mid-intermediate students.

The solutions to the problems set in some of the exercises are given in the Answers section on page 115.

The Bibliography on pages 117 and 118 gives some suggestions for further reading and details of the books referred to in the text.

If you are particularly interested in Community Language Learning look at section 11 on pages 106 to 111.

If you are involved in training teachers, then you should find section 12 on pages 112 to 114 of interest.

The Index on pages 119 to 121 is designed to help you to quickly find an exercise that is appropriate to your class.

Remember that all of these exercises are offered as starting points for your own invention. Read our suggestions *carelessly*, and thus create your own new ideas. Invite your students to come in on the act. This book will be most useful when you have forgotten all about it and dictation has become a part of your own personal repertoire.

The authors would be interested to hear of your experiences, triumphs and disasters. We would enjoy hearing about: dictations we have never dreamt of; exercises you have misread creatively; student reactions and inventions; staffroom reactions; text created by students; group dynamic developments; changes in attitudes – your students' and your own.

You can write to us at these addresses:

Paul Davis,   Mario Rinvolucri,
Eurocentres,   Pilgrims,
62, Bateman Street,   8, Vernon Place,
Cambridge, CB2 1LX   Canterbury, CT1 3YG
England.   England.

Tips for reading aloud

1 Whether sitting or standing, make sure your voice carries and does not disappear into the floor or table.
2 To stop you looking down at the table/floor, hold the book or paper up in front of you but not blocking your face. If you have squashed ribs because you're sitting or standing badly, you'll run out of breath: so make yourself comfortable.
3 If you have to turn a page during the reading, it can help to have the page you are going to turn ready before you start.
4 The correct volume to use depends on the size and shape of the room, the number of people in it and what you are reading. Rooms with lots of curtains or rooms full of people will absorb more sound. You'll need to compensate.
5 You should be easy to listen to and your listeners should not have to strain to hear. It's worth remembering though that reading in too

loud a voice can put people off. Your listeners should be drawn to you.

6 It's easy to read too fast. The listeners need time to absorb what is being read to them before they can make sense of the next bit, especially if they do not have a copy of the text.

7 It's important to pause: between changes in ideas; for dramatic effect; to make sense of dialogue, etc.

8 It helps to raise and lower your voice, again to show that a different character is speaking if there is dialogue in the text, or to indicate a change of mood, or when a new idea is being introduced. It's important to avoid monotony.

9 You can stress important words by increasing the power of your voice, or by lowering it so that students have to crane to hear. This can really help the listeners to make sense of what is being read.

10 If you can, make eye contact. This means looking up from what you are reading and looking at your listeners. The activity will become more personal as a result, it will give you the chance to put across the meaning of the text with the help of facial expressions, and it will mean that you will be able to gauge the listeners' reactions. If you are a beginner at this, practise the habit by looking up at the end of the last sentence of a paragraph. You will then have time to find your place in the text again as this is a natural place to pause.

11 Look interested in what you are reading. Enthusiasm and boredom are infectious.

12 It may be necessary to introduce briefly what you are going to read so that the listeners can place it in context.

13 If you make a mistake, don't stop or repeat yourself unless the mistake alters the meaning of the text. If you have to repeat it take your time, and make sure you get it right.

14 Of course, mistakes are less likely if you have made yourself familiar with the text before you use it in class.

Acknowledgement

Maggie Melville provided this section.

1 Correction

Much has been written in recent years about the necessary process by which learners work through their individual errors and their correction towards an increasingly accurate and fluent command of the language they are learning. Correcting is one of the teacher's major functions in any classroom, though it is a function which can be more or less positively performed.

In many situations the teacher corrects by modelling, for example:

Student: I had breakfast with a hamburger.
Teacher: You mean I had a hamburger for breakfast.

Notice how a more natural way of modelling would be for the teacher to imitate the behaviour of a parent with a small child and say:

Teacher: You mean you had a hamburger for breakfast.

In this section however, we do not deal with modelled corrections.

In 'Speed control' (page 12), students are given the chance to subordinate the teacher's reading pace to their writing pace and so produce more accurate text. In the other exercises correction is also conducted cooperatively. 'Saying it right' (page 13), for example, offers students the opportunity to correct their own pronunciation mistakes which the teacher has indicated in writing on the board. 'Grammar charts' (page 18), which owes its inspiration to the Silent Way, also focuses on correcting pronunciation in addition to working on grammar.

In normal circumstances, one person both creates and monitors the language produced. But in 'Shadow dictation' (page 14), 'Passing the buck' (page 16), and 'Word fields' (page 17), while one person both creates and monitors, i.e. writes down the dictation with care, a second person functions *solely* as a monitor. As a variation on this technique, 'Complete correction' (page 15) encourages students to continue monitoring after the creative process is complete.

Of course, students generally do their best to avoid mistakes or to self-correct when they produce English. The following exercises allow more room for this process, and are exciting to watch – the teacher can

Correction

learn a lot about her students' errors, and about the students themselves as individuals.

In all sections of this book, of course, correcting is to be seen in a variety of forms: in this section it is the focus of our attention.

1.1 Speed control

Usually it is the reader who controls the speed of the dictation. In this exercise, the writers dictate the speed they need and want.

Here is an example of a possible text. Explain any hard words in it. Then read the whole text through once at normal pace.

Terrible Revenge of a Lover

A Bergen citizen who several days a week drives a ready-mix cement truck as a second job, the other day came by his own residence and saw a friend's car with a sun-roof parked there. He stopped the cement truck and went in the apartment building to say hello. But sounds from the bedroom gave him to understand that it wasn't him but rather his wife that the fellow had come to visit. Without disturbing the couple in the bedroom, the man went back out of the building and over to his friend's car. He pulled the sun-roof back and backed the cement truck alongside it. Then he switched on the delivery system and filled the parked car with about two cubic metres of cement. When the lover came for his car the cement was completely hard. Later in the evening the car was towed away. The case has not been reported to the police.

(from *The Vanishing Hitch-hiker* by Jan H. Brunwand)

Now tell the students that they can control your reading. You will continue until someone calls out 'Stop'. Then you will be silent until someone calls out 'Go back to . . .'. You become the group's compliant cassette recorder!

Start reading and carry on until you are stopped. Don't start again until you are told to. The students must tell you where they want you to read from. Read at a natural, slow speed – this is different from 'dictating', in which you break up the text into listening chunks. Here you make breaks where the *listeners* ask you.

Finally, give out copies of the story so that students can compare what they have written with the original.

Acknowledgement

We learnt this technique from Seth Lindstromberg and Tessa Woodward.

1.2 Saying it right

If you have 10 students give out strips of paper with one sentence from the text below to each of them. Do not give the sentences out in order. If you have 20 people in the group give out one sentence to each pair, if 30, one sentence to each threesome, etc.

Gratitude

Peter worked as a night watchman in a smallish factory.
That morning the boss came in with a suitcase.
He told Peter he would be flying to New York the next day.
Peter immediately told him not to.
The factory owner asked why.
Peter told him that he had had a nightmare.
In his nightmare he had seen the next day's plane to New York crashing.
Peter's boss cancelled his ticket and didn't fly to New York.
The next day the plane crashed.
The boss thanked Peter and gave him a big present. He also sacked him.

© Cambridge University Press 1988

Answer any vocabulary questions that the students want to ask. Tell them that the bits of paper make a story and that the story includes a problem. Ask the students, around the class, to read out their sentences twice.

Ask the person or sub-group who thinks they have the first sentence in the story to dictate it to you at the board. Make sure that you write small enough to get all the sentences onto the board.

Take down exactly what is dictated. If a French student dictates, 'Ze boss asked Peter why', write it down like that. The student herself or those around are almost certain to want to correct this. Don't correct it on the board until the student has pronounced the word correctly. If a Spanish student turns the word 'asked' into two syllables, write it down that way, 'ask ed'. If a Greek student dictates 'crassed' instead of 'crashed' write it down her way.

The students dictate their sentences to you in what they think is the right order. When they see all the sentences up they may want to change the order – they can do this easily by numbering the sentences.

Once the order is established write up: 'Why the gift, the thanks and the sacking?'. Have them work on this in small groups.

Note

See page 115 for a likely answer.

1.3 Shadow dictation

This is a way of organising your students for an otherwise ordinary dictation so that they help each other and do their own correcting.

Pair* your students. One of each pair should sit behind a desk and be ready to write; the other should sit in front, facing you with her back to her partner, and be ready to listen carefully. Thus:

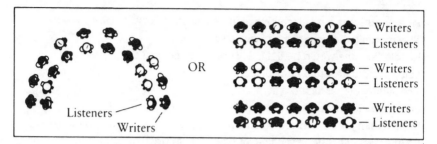

This seating arrangement helps the students to separate the activities; the listeners only *listen*, the writers have to *write*. Now read your text (any kind of text is suitable for this exercise). Do not let the 'listeners' have any paper or pens. If any of them object, offer them a swap with a student who would rather listen than write.

Maintain eye contact with the students who are *not* writing – help as necessary with mime, gesture and whisper. Encourage students to consult/help their partners as necessary. There will often be spontaneous consultation as the writers, who have two tasks to contend with, seek assistance from those who only have to listen. Pause as necessary to facilitate this.

When the dictation has finished the students who have not written should check the text of those who have. Don't give a definitive text as this will reduce the value of the correction work, but be available to answer any queries.

---

* Pair your students carefully. Quite often this exercise works better with the louder students writing and the quieter students as helpers/listeners. But there is a remedial possibility; you might like to try to get some of the weaker writers writing and some of the weaker listeners listening.

1.4 Complete correction

Select a short text like the one below:

Wally

He got up, got dressed, brushed his teeth and had a shower. Then he had to change out of his wet clothes. What a start to the day! He went out, got on his bike and started off but he'd forgotten his file so he had to turn back and get it. When he got back he found he'd left the shower on. What a mess! Now he had to clean it up.

Finally he got to school but when he got there he found everything was completely closed. It was a holiday.

What a wally!

Before reading this explain to the students that you'll read the text three, four, five, six times – as many times as they want. Explain that when they've finished and are satisfied with the text they will give it to you. Their job is then to listen carefully as you reread the text for others, and note any bits they have second thoughts about.

Read a first time. Read a second time. Read a third, fourth and fifth time. You may like to gradually increase the pace of delivery on successive readings. After each reading collect papers which the students are satisfied with. On each collection reaffirm, if necessary, that the students have a second task – 'just' to listen and reassess.

After five or six readings students will mostly have finished their writing and a majority will have finished their listening. Take in all the remaining papers and read the text through once more. Keep the pace of reading quick with the students listening once more to reassess.

Now give back the papers and ask for any questions. The 'post-dictation listening' will have focused the students' attention wonderfully – they will fire questions about spelling but also about meaning and grammar. Write answers quickly on the board or OHP.

1.5 Passing the buck

This is another exercise you can use with any text to encourage self-correction. It is particularly interesting in the way it avoids the impression that one student is being 'marked' by another.

Have the students sit in a tightish circle, or the nearest arrangement to this that your classroom will allow. Each student should have a blank sheet of paper and a pencil and rubber. Dictate the first sentence 'or phrase of the text.

Once the students have finished writing tell them to pass their paper to the student to their right. They then underline any mistakes they think they can see on the sheet they receive. They do not correct them.

Dictate the second sentence. Students again pass on their paper to their right when they have finished. This time students underline any mistakes in the second sentence but correct any mistakes in the first.

After giving the students enough time to think, dictate the third sentence. Make it clear that each time the students finish taking down a sentence they should pass the paper on and underline mistakes in the last sentence and correct the last but one sentence. In this way a natural rhythm of passing on, underlining and correcting should build up, avoiding hold-ups. Encourage any 'cheating', looking over shoulders or consultation that develops, as you are asking them to undertake a cooperative venture.

Finally the students can work alone or in small groups of neighbours correcting the text they have ended up with until they are satisfied that they have a correct text. Because the text written by each student is distributed over many sheets of paper this exercise is cooperative and non-judgemental.

1.6 Word fields [▢░░▢█▢░▢] ✓

It is possible to write interesting texts with word fields lifted from areas such as computing and medicine, even though the texts actually have nothing at all to do with computing or medicine. For example:

She wanted to *escape* for an hour or two so she decided to go for a *drive*.
When she got outside it was raining a *bit* so she had to *run* for the car . . .

This is an extract from a neutral, in fact rather ordinary text which contains the 'computer' words *escape*, *drive*, *bit* and *run*. The students can be set a secondary task of identifying the words associated with computers as they take down the normal dictation.

The longer example which follows comes from a lesson which was a direct response to a young upper-intermediate class where the boys were weak at writing and needed remedial work. They would normally have resented correction by their partners but the secondary task of word recognition (at which they were very good) reduced their anxiety about writing and improved their overall performance.

To use this exercise, pair students one girl to one boy (two girls to a boy is fine too). Explain that the boys are to write the text while the girls check/help. In the text, which is not connected with sport, there are over a dozen words which can be connected with sport (particularly foot-ball); the task is to identify these words and highlight them. Dictate each part once only, but give the pairs plenty of time to check and identify the sports words.

She sat in the corner pensively. She took a sip of her coffee and spat it out because it was so foul. Her goal that evening had been to finish her essay but there had been constant interruptions. For a start her boyfriend had dropped in. She'd heard him whistling as he came up the path and jumped up like a shot to let him in. But they'd had a row which had just made her very defensive. She had just put up what he called her wall, and been ready for every move he made. As she thought about it she tried to block the memory from her mind.

© Cambridge University Press 1988

After giving the students time to check, read the text again if necessary. Finally discuss the 'sports' words together. Some of them are closely connected with sport, others less so.

Notes

See page 115 for a likely answer.

Pairings other than the boy/girl, weak/strong one above are possible, for example young/old, scientist/artist, introvert/extrovert, etc. depending on your students and the word field chosen.

1.7 Grammar charts (from the Silent Way)

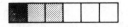

This lesson is designed for beginners whose mother tongue is an Indo-European language written in the Roman script. Make a grammar word chart on a large piece of cardboard/OHP transparency. Here is a possible chart:

to   this   them   because   a

and   as   has   me

it   which

am   and   two   I   get

not   an

do   had   here   does

him

there   one   her

is

you   their   did   but   are

have   us   mine   what

our   why   of   he

she   got   for   how

Go into class and ask the students to write down all the words they already know in English – you could well do this in the first class, as there are many situations round the world in which 'beginners' already know the odd word in English, through a song, film, advertising or borrowing into their own language. *Oter/lu* (hotel) is now a Japanese word, just as *le weekend* is French.

Once the students have had a chance to think on their own, ask them to work in small groups. Finally get a 'secretary' to write up on the board the words from everybody in the group. Copy these out yourself onto a large cardboard sheet or OHP transparency. Check that all of the meanings are known to everybody.

You now have a chart of content words known by the students, and a chart of grammar words that may be largely unknown to them.

Give a student a longish stick to point out the words. Ask her to tap out any sentence she can using words from either or both charts. If her sentence is wrong signal this to her without speaking. Once she has tapped a correct phrase or sentence ask someone in the group to read what she has just tapped. Work on the pronunciation silently, by getting the speaker to associate each syllable of the sentence with a finger on your hands. Then silently indicate the finger where the pronunciation problem lies. Using fingers like this you can silently work on stress and intonation too. Your silence creates a life-giving vacuum.

Using the two charts you may decide to tap out sentences that help students to start working on new words in the grammar chart. You may ask Student A in the group to make a sentence from the charts which Student B at the front with the stick should then tap out. Student B may tap out a sentence that the rest of the group writes down.

A student may come to the front and say a sentence from the charts, and then the others try to write it down. The student then taps it on the charts so that the others can check what they have written.

A student may come out and tap three words that don't make a sentence and the group should add other words to make these first three into an acceptable sentence. For example, if the student taps *two*, *had* and *but*, this could become *Two girls had a boyfriend but no father*, etc.

Once you get used to working with the charts you will find that many more manipulation exercises will occur to you spontaneously, guided by the needs of a particular group. All of the above techniques can be used in fluid combination with each other.

Note

The idea of working with charts comes from Caleb Gattegno's Silent Way. You can make the work suggested above both more sophisticated and more powerful by using the word charts designed for teaching Silent

Way. These charts are colour-coded so that, for example, the schwa sound /ə/ in <u>a</u>mazing, vist<u>a</u>, mast<u>er</u>ly p<u>er</u>form<u>a</u>nce, etc. is the same colour in all its spellings. All the spellings of a given sound are systematically listed on a second range of charts called 'Fidels' or phonic/spelling charts. The use of charts created by the students themselves is, however, affectively more powerful.

You can read more about the Silent Way in these books: *Memory, Meaning and Method* and *A Way and Ways* by Earl Stevick; and *Teaching Foreign Languages in Schools the Silent Way* and *The Common Sense of Teaching Foreign Languages* by Caleb Gattegno. All of these books are listed in the Bibliography on page 117.

To use the Silent Way approach fully, which means in some cases a radical change in the way you relate to a group of students, you need training. For more information contact:

Educational Explorers,
11, Crown Street,
Reading,
England.

Educational Solutions,
95, University Place R.4555,
New York, NY 10003,
USA.

Pronunciation charts by Adrian Underhill based on the Silent Way approach are available from:

Adrian Underhill,
International House,
White Rock,
Hastings,
East Sussex TN35 1JP,
England.

In this book, 'Adjectives' (page 76), and 'Before and after' (page 77) are also based on the Silent Way approach.

2 Sounds, spellings and punctuation

In teaching a language like Spanish or German where there is a closer match between spelling and pronunciation, the exercises in this section would not be necessary. But English is a mishmash of influences: Germanic grammar, Danish and French vocabulary, Renaissance borrowings from Greek and Latin, later imperial borrowings and Americanisms. The relative simplicity of the structure of English, for example its lack of inflections and of gender, may not always be obvious to a learner struggling with the vagaries of the written form. To take an extreme example: a student who hears the sound /s/ during a dictation can write *s, ss, se, 's, c, ce, sc, st, sw, ps, sce, sse, sch, sth*, or even *tz* depending on the word and still get it right!*

The exercises in this section concentrate on different aspects of the speaking or writing of English. These include letters which are not sounded: 'Silent letter' (page 22); the spelling and pronunciation of past endings: 'Past endings' (page 23); the effect on English pronunciation of a student's first language: 'Interference' (page 24); syllable structure and stress within words: 'Listening for word stress' (page 25); punctuation and other features: 'Firing questions' (which gives a fully worked example of an approach to dictating text) (page 26); and punctuation through attention to the accuracy needed in computer programming: 'Program punctuation' (page 27).

For a divergent nineteenth-century view see page 122.

---

* u*s*, pa*ss*, promi*se*, Dick'*s*, reci*te*, on*ce*, *s*cience, li*s*ten, *sw*ord, *p*salm, acquie*sce*, fine*sse*, *sch*ism, is*th*mus, and wal*tz*.
This list is based on the American English Silent Way Fidel (see page 20).

Sounds, spellings and punctuation

2.1 Silent letter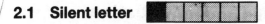

Write *answer* and *listen* on the board. Ask the students to suggest which letters are silent and underline them. Dictate the following words with the students taking them down and underlining the letters which are silent. The words should be ones they are already mostly familiar with.

sand̲wich	hal̲f	whist̲le
crum̲b	wal̲k	boug̲ht
k̲nee	w̲rong	bom̲b
Christ̲mas	foreig̲n	chal̲k

Pause and have the students check with their neighbours and/or dictionaries and finally by reading them back to you.

Now continue the dictation. This time, instead of writing the words, ask the students to write the number of letters in the word and the silent letter or letters.

plum̲ber	cup̲board	daug̲hter
coul̲d	g̲uitar	sig̲n
cal̲m	c̲haracter	h̲onest
thum̲b	w̲rap	yac̲ht

Have the students compare and reach a consensus. Continue with a discussion about their feelings about the differences between spelling and pronunciation in English.

Note

The most obvious 'silent letters' have been marked in the examples above, but students will often point out others.

2.2 Past endings 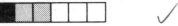 ✓

Explain that for most English verbs the past ending in writing is *-ed*, but that this has three distinct pronunciations in British English. Ask the students to make three columns each headed by one of the appropriate transcriptions 'T', 'D' and 'ID'. (You may want to use the phonetic transcription from the dictionary they use, probably /t/, /d/ and /ɪd/.) Then feed them three examples (e.g. *pushed, pulled, started*) to mull over; notice that all of these are easily mimed. Give the students as many repeat hearings as they ask for at this stage. Soon the students should have:

T	D	ID
/t/	/d/	/ɪd/
pushed	pulled	started

Select about 20 verbs you think the students know and enjoy from the list below, and dictate them with their past ending, asking students to write them in the appropriate column. Give each word once only. If further hearings are needed, elicit them from the students. If they don't understand a verb then mime it.

Remember that the distinction between /t/ (voiceless) and /d/ (voiced) shows up best with a following vowel, so you may find it useful to say transitive verbs in front of *it* and intransitive verbs in front of *again* – *washed it, listened again*, etc.

opened	closed	washed	danced	remembered
listened	talked	phoned	snored	hated
laughed	cried	hoped	patted	folded
groaned	copied	screamed	clapped	wished
played	breathed	needed	smoked	puffed
offered	refused	liked	walked	worked
cleaned	called	mended	landed	jumped
hopped	needed	missed	hoped	rained

Have the students compare their columns and correct any spelling errors. Ask them to look up the suffix *-ed* in a good dictionary. It will explain, and you can add to this if you wish, that after /p/, /k/, /f/, /θ/, /s/, /ʃ/, and /tʃ/, *-ed* is pronounced /t/, and that after /t/ and /d/ it is pronounced /ɪd/ (/əd/ in American English), but that after all other sounds, including vowels, it is pronounced /d/.

Finally, have the students dictate the words back to you. You write them in appropriate columns on the board, either as they should be, or as you have been given them (for correction).   ⫸→

Variation 1

Dictate the verbs without the endings, which the students must supply.

Variation 2

Repeat the task with the plural endings (/s/, /z/, /ɪz/).

2.3 Interference

Play the students a tape of two or three varieties of regional accent or the accents of different nationalities of native English speakers – British, American, Indian, Australian, etc. (These are available on the tapes to the *Cambridge English Course* or the *Strategies* series, or you might like to record them yourself using a few colleagues.) Ask the students to pick out three differences from the English they are normally taught.

Invite each student to think of a sentence, for example a simple request. In turn they record the sentences on your tape recorder, first in their mother tongue and then in English.

Ask the students to make two columns on a piece of paper, and, as they listen to the tape to 'draw' the intonation pattern of their mother tongue in the first column and of English in the second, and to write down any other features that are noticeably different. Play back the whole tape – the mother tongue and the English versions – pausing after each pair of sentences.

After the students have made their notation for a pair of sentences, give them time to comment, particularly on the way their first language interferes with English. (By asking them to record their own language first you are, in effect, inviting interference.)

If you have a class with different mother tongues, have the students with the same first language in sequence on the tape, so that they can recognise the common forms of interference.

This exercise improves group cohesion by:

– sanctioning the sound of other languages in the English classroom
– encouraging students to enjoy the sound of another person's language
– making students aware of other language users' difficulties in English.

Note

Students should choose their own way of 'drawing', although they will, of course, use any previous knowledge they have of representing language. This exercise works well with students accustomed to Community Language Learning (see page 106).

2.4 Listening for word stress [ ] [ ] [ ] [ ]

Have everybody say their first name in turn. Ask the group to say how many syllables each name has and where (in names of more than one syllable) the stress lies.

Now choose some 'international' words, model the English version and have the students say how many syllables each has and where the stress lies. For example, the following words are fairly international or understandable at any level – at least for speakers of Indo-European languages: *fantastic, photograph, engineer, kangaroo.* Then have the students pronounce the words in their mother tongue and indicate the number of syllables and the stress.

Now have the students make two columns on a piece of paper. Dictate a selection of two-syllable English words which the students have come across lately in class. Ask them to put those with first syllable stress in the left-hand column and those with second syllable stress on the right. For example:

forty	canteen
coffee	(a) cassette
(a) record	(to) record

Have them check with a good dictionary. (You may need to explain the convention used to show stress, usually: '*happy.*)

Repeat with three columns for three-syllable words. For example:

syllable	computer	cigarette

Ask the students for homework to prepare a list of two- or three-syllable words connected with their work or hobby: these should be put in columns according to where the stress falls. Next lesson you can repeat the exercise, with students dictating to each other in pairs.

2.5 Firing questions

Firing questions at students to check their spelling and understanding of meaning is a simple way of making a dictation more active for the students. Two simple ways of doing this are to ask a question at the end of a sentence, e.g. 'How many words are there in this sentence?', or to stop dictating and ask for the next word or bit of punctuation. It's important to use your voice to distinguish when you are dictating and when you are asking a question as an aside. We have sometimes used a teacherish voice for the dictation and an urgent informal tone for the asides. Head movements help too. It's essential to allow the students enough time to take down fully the bit of dictation they are concerned with before butting in with the aside.

A: Something awful's happened! (What's the *'s* mean?)
B: What? (What's the punctuation?)
A: I've lost my keys. (What's the opposite of *lost?*)
B: Are you sure? (What's the punctuation?)
A: 'Course I am. (What could be before *'course?*) **They've completely** (Stop after *completely* and ask for the next word.) **disappeared. I've looked everywhere.**
B: Are they in your bag? (What's the difference between *bag* and *purse?*)
A: No. I've taken every (Stop after *every* and ask for the second half of the word.) **thing out and . . .**
B: What about the car? (Stop here and ask for the next sentence.) **Have you looked there?**
A: Yes. I've completely cleared out the front and (Stop after *and.* Mime *feel* and ask for the right word – and the past tense.) **felt all down the backs of the seats.**
B: Have you tried the bedroom?
A: Uh huh. I've looked all over the house. (How many words are there in the second sentence? – Contractions count as two.)
B: Well . . . where have you been today? (How many letters are there in the fifth word? What's the punctuation?) **Think!** (What's the punctuation?) **You must've dropped them somewhere.**
A: I haven't (Stop after *haven't* and ask for the next word.) **been anywhere – just shopping in Sainsbury's.** (How many letters are there in the last but two word?)
B: Have you phoned them (What's *them?*) **up to see if some** (Stop after *some* and ask what comes next) **one's handed them in?**
A: No, I haven't. I'll do it now.

This is a simple technique for jazzing up a boring textbook dialogue – if the text is gripping the interruptions would be intrusive. Reading through the dialogue before the lesson will suggest the questions you can use. When you are asking the students to predict, make sure the next bit of text is easily predictable.

Acknowledgement

The text above was adapted from one written by Larry Cole. We came across the simple idea of asking students how many words there are in a sentence to check listening in the *Cambridge English Course* by Michael Swan and Catherine Walter.

2.6 Program punctuation

More and more students are becoming familiar with computers and computer programming. And one of the features of programs is that they must be exactly right – otherwise they simply don't work.

Dictate the following short BASIC program to a class of post-beginner/elementary students, or print out or photocopy enough copies so that one student can dictate to another student at the keyboard. The program will work on any make of computer with a few changes (it is written in BBC BASIC), but check with your local human-being-friendly buff if in doubt – and try it out in advance!

Before dictating you may need to pre-teach the following: space, return (i.e. new line), open/close inverted commas, question mark, capital/small letters, apostrophe, $ (i.e. string), INPUT.

```
10 PRINT "What's your name?"
20 INPUT name$
30 PRINT "What's the number of your house and
the name of your road?"
40 INPUT street$
50 PRINT "What's the name of your town or city?"
60 INPUT city$
70 PRINT "What's your postcode?"
80 INPUT code$
90 PRINT "What's your phone number?"
100 INPUT P$
110 CLS
120 PRINT name$
130 PRINT street$
140 PRINT city$
150 PRINT code$
160 PRINT P$
```

⟩⟩⟩→

27

B

Sounds, spellings and punctuation

When the students have finished ask them to type RUN. If the students have made absolutely no mistakes the computer will ask them to feed in their name and address and phone number and will print it neatly on the screen. If the student has, say, missed a set of inverted commas or put a space in the wrong place the program will 'crash' and the computer will print 'Mistake at line 40' or some such. When this happens stress that the computer is very stupid and needs precise instructions, and hand out copies of the program for them to correct. (Press ESCAPE and then LIST to get the program back on the screen.) Computers need totally accurate punctuation to function. Note that BBC BASIC will not accept commas as punctuation, so '24, Christchurch St.' should be written as '24 Christchurch St.'.

Many students are at least semi computer literate and so will probably not feel anxious about fiddling with computers.

At secondary school level, try splitting your class into single-sex groups; the problems of boys not working well with girls are sometimes exaggerated by the presence of a computer.

If you are new to computers then make sure to type in the program a couple of times yourself. Keep a note of any snags you encounter so as to be able to 'trouble shoot' when trying it out with a group.

Glossary

This Glossary may help, but remember that some of the information may vary with the make of computer.

RETURN – this tells the computer to carry on. At the end of each instruction or process the computer will wait for you to press the RETURN key before it continues.

INPUT – the computer will ask you to *put* something *in* the computer (in this case a name, street, town, etc.).

$ (string) – computers cannot understand words. So every time you feed a word/words new to the computer you have to tell it that it's a word (literally a string of letters) by giving this symbol.

CLS – tells the computer to clear the screen.

RUN – tells the computer to start the program.

CRASH – this is when the program fails because of some error.

ESCAPE/LIST – if the program has crashed, press the ESCAPE key to get out of the program. Then type LIST which will give you the program on the screen.

Acknowledgement

The program was originally suggested by Sara Bennett.

3 The telephone

Telephone conversations are frequently accompanied by some form of writing activity. You jot down the time, the place, the room number or the address the other person has given you; you are forced to get the other person to spell names for you; you may find yourself writing out a message for a colleague. You are specially careful, as details must not be taken down wrongly. In other words, dictations and semi-dictations are a normal part of working with the telephone.

This section proposes realistic practice, mostly using real phones. This accustoms the students to dealing with the reduced and distorted sound of the human voice when heard over the phone, and to the fact that not being seen means that as a language learner you may get less sympathetic consideration from the native speaker. It also helps students who dislike using a phone in any language to come to terms with the instrument.

Particular exercises cope with particular difficulties: 'Quick calls' (page 31) focuses on numbers, which are a notoriously hard area even for some advanced speakers. 'Instant lesson' (page 34) helps students to visualise spatial directions they might be given over the phone. 'Seeking information' (page 33) practises just what you would expect.

This section is particularly useful for students doing business and commercial English courses.

3.1 Taking a message

This activity is a confidence builder for students who have never used English over the phone. Pre-teach useful phone language, such as:

Is there a message for me?
Can you spell the first/second/nth word?
What was that again?
Sorry, I didn't catch that.
Let me read it back.
Was that . . .?

Ask the students to phone you at home one evening, say between six and seven o'clock, to get a message. When they do so, dictate one of the sentences from the 'split story' below, and tick off their name on your list. The students' job is to note down the sentence accurately and, having written it down, memorise it for the next day. Don't be overly helpful on the phone – if they don't understand, wait for them to ask you to repeat or spell a word.

In the next lesson the students can put the story together. If the odd student hasn't managed to get her sentence, check your list and feed the missing sentence in.

The story below has 16 sentences. By amalgamating sentences or adding new ones you can make it suitable for larger or smaller groups. If you have around 30 students in your group the story construction could take place in two parallel groups. When the students ring up you note down their names in two separate lists, and in the next class simply read out the lists to form the groups.

A man and his son had been to a party.
They were driving back together.
They had had a very good time.
It was raining and the road was wet.
A cat was crossing the road.
The man swerved to avoid the cat.
The car skidded on the wet road.
It crashed into a tree.
The man was killed.
His son was seriously injured.
Someone called for an ambulance.
It rushed the son to hospital.
He was immediately taken to the operating theatre.
The surgeon washed and went into the theatre.
The surgeon saw the boy and shouted, 'My son! My son!'
Can you explain?

© Cambridge University Press 1988

Variation

If you are teaching in an English-speaking environment, prime a nice helpful receptionist/secretary. Students phone the school at a pre-arranged period of their free time to ask for a message (one to two hours is enough time for them all to get through). The secretary gives them one sentence each from the split story and ticks their name off the list so you can check the odd student who doesn't have time to get through. You might decide, if your school agrees, to ask them to make a reverse/transferred charge call (in American English, to call collect). This way they have to go through the operator, which creates additional language demands.

Note

See page 115 for a possible solution to the story.

Acknowledgement

Katie Head suggested this exercise. Thanks to Rebecca Seward and Joanna Webb for taking an awful lot of phone calls!

3.2   Quick calls

Counting is one thing, 'giving one's number' is quite another. There is a world of difference between 2,176,490 (counting) and 217-6490 (phone number). This exercise gives practice in this area. You will probably need to look at the notes below to explain what you have always taken for granted yourself.

Write your phone number on the board. Ask the students to shout out their phone numbers – you write them on the board as they do so. When they all have their numbers on the board, go through splitting numbers into stress groups (see *Note*), and have the students repeat individually or in groups. Get the rhythm right.

Adjourn to the school office/staffroom or any place you can find access to two phone extensions out of sight of each other. Have the students form two groups at the two extensions. Open the line. The first student at extension A says her phone number, the first at extension B notes it down and says it aloud to the other members of the group, and vice versa. Repeat this with subsequent pairs.

Back in the classroom check by taking down the numbers on the board, and then explain that students are to phone each other that evening and exchange addresses. In a later lesson, they could check the addresses with each other.

In a non-English environment the students can give fictitious names and addresses. Many students like the fantasy element. You can brainstorm typical English family names, first names, street names and towns on the board. Each student then publicly takes on a new identity. This can be useful later for role play.

Note

To a certain extent, native speakers of British English seem to have individual preferences as to how they say phone numbers. These are general guidelines:

1 Each digit is stressed and said individually. *1234567* becomes *one two three//four five//six seven*.
2 Numbers with an even number of digits are split into groups of two or three: *one two three // four five six*, or *one two // three four // five six*. The latter is often preferred when exceptional clarity is required, say over a bad line.
3 Numbers with an odd number of digits are split into groups of three and two: *one two // three four five*, or, less usually, *one two three // four five*.
4 If the same number occurs twice in succession then it is not usually repeated. *11* becomes *double one*; *111* becomes either *one double one*, or, less usually, *treble one*.
5 *Double* is used wherever possible, and so influences the choice of grouping. *122345* becomes *one double two // three four five*, rather than *one two // two three // four five*; and *123345* becomes *one two // double three // four five*, rather than *one two three // three four five*.
6 Symmetry influences groupings. *121343* becomes *one two one // three four three*; *12334* becomes *one two // double three four*.
7 Codes form a separate group. *0638-123456* becomes *oh six three eight // one two three // four five six*.
8 Remember that the pronunciation of *0* is usually 'oh' in telephone numbers.

3.3 Telephone tree

Write your name on the board. Ask two students to volunteer their phone numbers; write their names and telephone numbers under yours. Ask four more students to give their telephone numbers. Write their names and telephone numbers under the others. Repeat with eight, etc. until you have a 'telephone tree' which includes all the class.

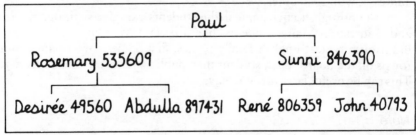

Explain that you will phone the first two people on the tree and dictate a sentence. The two should then add one word to the sentence and phone up the two students under them on the tree. This carries on, with each student adding a word. The expanded sentence must still make sense.

Your original sentence should be as sparse and simple as possible to allow for expansion. Be prepared for it to grow in strange directions!

Show how a tree might progress thus:

Property is theft.
Property is really theft.
Property isn't really theft.
Stealing property isn't really theft.
Stealing property isn't really serious theft.
etc.

Now ask each student to suggest a good time for her to be reached. Write it by her name.

Give the group a weekend to get through. At the next lesson they report back on how their sentence grew along the branches.

3.4 Seeking information

The following text is suitable for use in Cambridge, but could easily be adapted to other towns. It can be done either in school as group work if you have enough extensions and outside lines, or individually as homework.

You're going to London at the weekend. Decide what time you're planning to set off, and approximately what time you're going to come back. (Decide where you're going first and work out whether Liverpool Street or King's Cross station is more convenient.) Look up Passenger Enquiries or the Talking Timetable in the phone book and take down the times of the best trains for you using the phone in the office (dial 9 for an outside line).

Use the phone to find out:
The opening times of the central library and whether you can borrow books.
What you can see in Saffron Walden this weekend.
Whether you can fly direct from Cambridge to Paris, Amsterdam or Edinburgh.
What the weather is like in London.
Today's recipe.

© Cambridge University Press 1988

Have the students report the information from their notes to the group on completion. It's also interesting to have them report back on the attitude of the people they talked to (if they weren't listening to recorded messages).

It is interesting to discuss whether they find it easier to get information from people or recordings. The latter are often clearer – but you can't ask for clarification or partial repetitions. This can lead into a useful discussion of conversational techniques.

Although these suggestions refer to work in Britain, a similar exercise is possible in many large cities around the world. Tasks could include ringing the consulate of an English-speaking country to find out about visa requirements, ringing airlines for flight times, ringing local British or American churches to find service times, and so on.

3.5 Instant lesson

The most interesting text for dictation often comes from immediate experience. It becomes an authentic communication by the teacher to the students of facts they need to know. At seminars many teachers have said they give short 'instant' dictations to initiate discussions or generally focus students at the beginning of lessons. It is often necessary for teachers to give out small pieces of information or instructions, and at the beginning of a lesson a short dictation is an excellent way of settling the students. In this type of exercise it is a good idea to allow the students one or two questions at the end of each sentence.

The following dictation was a direct response to students, and is typical of a telephone message. At the end of term Paul had invited a group for a party. His house is notoriously difficult to find but the students by now knew the streets of Cambridge pretty well. So . . .

You're at the main entrance of the school. Turn right. Go to the end of the street and turn left into Hills Road and keep going until you get to the traffic lights near the Catholic church. Cross Hills Road and go diagonally across Parker's Piece until you can see a white arch to your right. Cross over the road and go through the arch into a little alleyway and keep on going. When you get to the end of the alley keep going until you get to a dead end. Turn right and then sharp left into City Road. Go straight on until you get to the main entrance of the Grafton Centre. Keep going past the entrance and you'll see an alley next to the bank. Go down the alley, turn left at the end and go through some car barriers. You should be able to see a red staircase near some bike sheds. Go up two flights of stairs to the first floor. At the top of the staircase go straight on and you'll see two doors opposite. Knock hard on the right-hand one. The exact address is 24, Christchurch Street. The telephone number is 36411.

The students checked their dictations together, and those who had maps checked with maps.

Variation

It is easy to replicate instant dictations of this kind even if you have nothing specific to announce. You could, for example, ask your students to suggest a place they know, an object, two names and a line of dialogue. Write them on the board. Around the words suggested you can improvise a dictation, building in – or using as a climax – the line of dialogue you have been given.

4 Single word dictations

This section deals with vocabulary and offers you a variety of revision and deepening exercises. 'Deepening' needs explaining. When a student first meets a word in a foreign language the meeting is superficial. Even if the student is able to translate the word correctly she still knows little about it and has little feeling for it. Several meetings are needed in different spoken and written contexts before the word starts to *belong* to the student and then to *become part of* the student.

The deepening process can take many forms. In 'Connections' (below), 'Collocations' (page 36), 'Word sets' (page 40) and 'Picking your words' (page 43) you will find different ways of helping the students to explore semantic fields. In 'The senses' (page 39) students are invited to notice how they perceive words through sight, sound, touch, taste and smell. In 'Words change' (page 37) students hazard a guess as to how they think English words will change over the next 20 years. 'Sounds American' (page 38) focuses on the differences between British and American English vocabulary.

4.1 Connections

Explain to the students that you are going to dictate some lists of words or phrases for them to write down. The items on each list are connected to each other in one, and only one, way. The students may see other ways early on in the dictation – accept these if they are valid but carry on, explaining that you have another common factor in mind. If at any time they think they are able to make the connection then they should shout out and explain. Only after the students have successfully connected the words should spelling or meaning be checked.

This works well as a review activity. The order in which the words are given makes a considerable difference to the difficulty in making the connection.

Dictate the first group as an example then continue with the others:

Wings, Byrds, Eagles, Police, Queen, Doors, Wham, Shadows, Genesis, Meatloaf, Stones, Beatles (pop groups)

picture, turn over, button, soap, interference, channel, zigzag, presenter, aerial, news (television)

byte, bit, bug, drive, ram, run, boot, load, screen, escape, disk (computers)
tear, lick, line, love, open, class, box, yours, stamp (post)
book, wire, pip, tone, sparrow*, code, buzz, pole, slot, booth, red (phone)
wall, water, stand, newspaper, house, private, paper, think, smallest, sit, flush,
    chain, bog (toilet)
cup, tray, make-up, cramped, VIP, bar, tax, free, inflate, handle (air travel/air
    hostess)
preparation, health, bottle, three times, prescribe, teaspoonful, a day (chemist)
money, people, experience, missing, relax, sabbatical, agent, brochure (travel)
appearance, spoon, hot, clean, disgusting, throw up, decoration, art, taste
    (cooking)
life, travel, Sun, salesman, dotted line, car, security, signature, policy (insurance)
wall, paper, road, colour, country, measure, find, far, book, equator (map)
clip, duplicate, safe, ribbon, cabinet, punch, enquiry, file (office)
target, agent, produce, cost, table, graph, tax, increase, rep (sales)

© Cambridge University Press 1988

Now have the students, working individually, create their own word
lists around a topic or theme of their own. They should dictate their lists
to the whole group (or sub-group). Each word should be written down
to provide thinking time and the chance for mental review. When a
theme is guessed the student stops and the rest of the group brainstorms
other words which could complete the set.

4.2 Collocations

This exercise draws on technical language and if you are teaching ESP
can be adapted to the needs of more or less any group of students. This is
a nice exercise to turn over to the students in their own specialities. But
of course it can be used for general English too.

Dictate the groups of words in the list below. Ask the students to give
the first noun they can think of which fits with each of the adjectives in
the set.

high, low, intermediate (technology)
thermal, daisywheel, dot-matrix, laser (printer)
solar powered, battery powered, mains, scientific (calculator)
hydraulic, pneumatic, manual, mechanical (steering)
hard, 3″, floppy (disk)
induction, compression, ignition, exhaust (process)
slip, pressure (gauge)
liquid crystal, digital (display)
high level, low level, programming (language)

© Cambridge University Press 1988

* Busby, who advertises British Telecom, is a sparrow.

Note

The *Lexicon of Contemporary English* by Tom McArthur is a good source of material for you or your students to get examples from.

4.3 Words change

Suggest to the class that a verb like 'dial' used to be an accurate term when most phones had dials rather than buttons. The word may survive but it describes something that is an increasingly obsolete activity as push-button phones take over. The word is undergoing a change of meaning.

Other words have virtually disappeared because what they refer to has already disappeared. We no longer have streetlamp lighters so the term has vanished. When the first American spacecraft returned to our planet, people used to talk about 'splashdown': the word has died with the change in technology and practice. We still remember transistors, but for how much longer?

Ask students to take these words down in the appropriate column:

obsolete in 2010 | changed meaning in 2010 | same as today in 2010

The students have to decide what is likely to happen to the words and the things they refer to over the next 20 or so years.

suitcase   information technology
assembly line   royalty   bus conductor
apprentice   arms race   customise
hi-jack   blacksmith   walkman
National Health Service   conservation
milkman   tea-bag   born-again
ghetto   Shi'ite   wedding
clutch   factory farm   blackboard
wholefood   package holiday   garage
soap opera   injection   plough
monetarism   tennis   pornography
ticket   racism   zoo   record player
traffic jam   star wars   tailor
printer   mugging   AIDS   telescope

Acknowledgement

This exercise was shown to us by John Morgan, co-author of *Vocabulary*.

4.4 Sounds American

As a warm-up, ask your students to suggest any differences they have noticed between American and British English.

Write a few pairs of words or phrases in random order on the board and ask the students to say which words mean the same and which is American and which British English. For example:

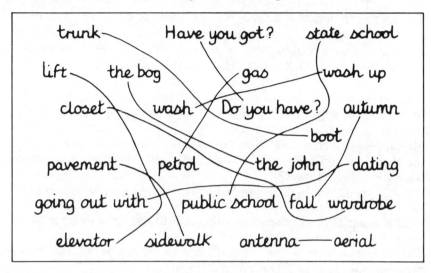

Dictate the following text. Tell the students that at the end they'll be asked to turn it into British English.

```
Dear Bonnie,
        Just finished my Masters and now in London for a vacation.
I've gotten myself a neat apartment close to the subway. I didn't
meet up with my old High School buddies yet but I met a nice
English girl across the hall. She fixed me lunch today and we're
taking in a show tonight.
            Do take care
                    Love *
```

Read the text through again if necessary and set the students the task of 'translating'. Remind them to change proper names.

Variation

Make an American English tape of the text and a British English one. Ask the students to divide into two groups according to whether they

---

* Ask students to write a typical American name here. Ask students what their typical American names are.

'feel' more American or British. Have the two groups transcribe the appropriate tape, 'translate' it into the language they 'feel' more for, and then compare texts.

Notes

See page 115 for some suggested equivalents.

In a mixed nationality class in the UK this exercise works expecially well with people from other parts of the Americas, Japanese/Koreans or students who have travelled in the States, because of their greater exposure to American English. But most students are interested because when they are travelling or working they are exposed to at least as much American as British English.

Acknowledgement

Thanks to Anne Matthews and Joanne Warren for providing the American text above.

4.5   The senses

This technique is excellent if you want to get the students to revise a largish group of mainly non-abstract words.
   The students need four columns on the page in front of them, with these headings:

   I see | I hear | I taste/smell | I feel through my body*

Tell them you are going to dictate a series of words. They are to take them down in the column that corresponds to their first sensory impression. Suppose the first word dictated is *cat*, some people may first 'see' a cat, others may 'hear' it purring, some will 'smell' the idea and others may 'feel' themselves stroking the cat (last column).

* This column excludes the other senses.

Single word dictations

Here are some words you could dictate:

computer	anchor	rabbit
church	cloud	beyond
pie	glue	yesterday
horse	toe-nail	hill
ink	oil	radio
Mary	God	fish
octopus	frame	vomit
violin	limp	paper clip
old	gurgle	afraid
shoes	rain	sing
dead	poke	freedom fighter
wood	fat	typewriter

Students are normally curious to compare their categorisation with that of others.

To round off the exercise it is interesting to find out how many people had a preponderance of words in one or two categories and which they were. You may find that you have a class of mainly visual (column 1) or kinaesthetic (column 4) students.

Acknowledgement

We learnt this exercise from Bernard Cleveland, author of *Master Teaching Techniques*. His work in turn is based on the brilliant and innovative studies of Richard Bandler and John Grinder, whose books include *TRANCEformations: Neuro-Linguistic Programming*, and *The Structure of Magic*.

4.6 Word sets

This selective dictation technique can be used with a range of texts at all levels from post-beginner to post-proficiency.

Prepare for the lesson by making sure that you can read the passage you have chosen fluently. Decide where you will pause for breath and for eye contact with the students. Reading aloud well is quite hard. (See pages 9–10 in the Introduction.)

An example text is given on page 41. Tell the students that their task while you read is to pick out all the words they hear connected with music and write them down. Then read the text.

Ask the students, in groups of three, to compare their lists.

Give them copies of the text to see if they have missed any music words and if there are any words they don't understand.

Sullivan's lost chords to be played again

by Norman Lebrecht

The only concerto composed by Sir Arthur Sullivan, believed lost after its destruction in a publisher's fire, has been reconstructed from memory by a conductor 32 years after its last performance.

The concerto, for cello and orchestra, dates from 1866, when Sullivan was 24 years old and regarded at home and abroad as the finest serious composer Britain had produced since Purcell. He had five years to go before joining the acid-tongued barrister W.S. Gilbert.

Sullivan wrote the concerto for the eminent Italian cellist, Alfredo Piatti, himself something of a composer. But after giving its premiere at Crystal Palace on November 24, 1866, and a further performance in Edinburgh, Piatti inexplicably dropped the work.

No rival rushed to retrieve it. Apart from an amateur rendition in Westminster in 1887, the concerto was not heard again until a young Australian conductor, Charles Mackerras, persuaded the BBC to accept it for broadcast in 1953. The soloist was William Pleeth, and the concerto was warmly received – 'not as a great unknown work', says Mackerras (now Sir Charles Mackerras), 'but as a very charming one'.

The composer's biographer, Arthur Jacobs, confirms this view. 'Since Sullivan did not revise it in later life as he did other youthful works,' he says, 'I have always felt this meant he did not think too much of the concerto.'

The concerto was never sent to the printer. When the original parts that Mackerras used perished in a fire at Chappell's, the music publishers, in 1964, Sullivan enthusiasts were distraught. Although hardly any broadcast concerts were recorded in those days, rumours that a tape had been circulated by the BBC's transcription service sent them scurrying fruitlessly through the archives.

Their distress was briefly relieved when Piatti's own score turned up at the Pierpoint Morgan Library in New York soon after the Chappell's fire. But it contained only the soloist's melodic line, without harmony, orchestration or ensemble passages. Implored at the time to undertake a painstaking restoration, Mackerras could not spare the time in a busy international career.

The work remained untouched until last year, when Julian Lloyd Webber, desperate like most cello soloists to expand the instrument's concert repertoire, convinced a publisher to take it on. A conductor, David Mackie, was engaged to write new orchestrations. He took his finished effort to Mackerras, who, condemned to idleness by a bout of hepatitis, suddenly found himself recalling long stretches of music that he had conducted once, half a lifetime before.

'The more I looked at it,' says Mackerras, 'the more I remembered. It sounds like a good 19th-century cello concerto.'

He does not claim absolute fidelity to the original, but believes the new score comes near enough to keep Sullivan's name on the title page.

(from *The Sunday Times* 5 July 1986)

Single word dictations

Here is another sample text. This time the words are not linked by topic but by general concept. Ask your students to write down all the words that have 'negative force'.

CIA Director fails to quell US suspicions

From Alex Brummer and Michael White in Washington

President Reagan's efforts to restore his credibility and put the Iran-Contra scandal behind him were floundering last night as the CIA director, Mr William Casey, joined a procession of Reagan aides who have failed to satisfy Congressional investigators of his proclaimed innocence.

There is growing concern among Reagan friends and critics as well as America's allies abroad, that unless the President acts quickly to bring out all the facts Congress's own inquiries will drag on well into the spring, crippling the Presidency in a welter of rumour and revelation. Yesterday produced yet more.

Although the hearings were held in camera, a succession of Congressmen of both parties emerged in front of a battery of television lights to offer a partial and often conflicting account of the proceedings. Representative Stephen Solarz, an up-and-coming Democrat, reported that in his opinion the 'higher authority' everyone was blaming in the affair was 'the President of the United States'.

He was contradicted by a Republican. 'No evidence we have heard would link the President to any of these illegal activities,' said Mr Mike Dewine of Ohio. A senior Republican, Mr William Bromfield, who is now urging the granting of immunity from criminal prosecution to key witnesses, said the three-hour session with Mr Casey had revealed 'serious errors of judgement by senior CIA personnel'.

Another Democrat spoke of Mr Casey having 'a tough memory problem'.

The President's loss of authority among the American people was emphasised yesterday by new opinion surveys showing that half the population believe that Mr Reagan is lying over what he knew about the diversion of the fund to the Contras.

Even though the voters still regard Mr Reagan as having more honesty and integrity than most public figures the steps he has taken to clean up his national security apparatus have not restored his approval ratings.

(from *The Guardian* 11 December 1986)

Note

The reaction of one French university colleague to this exercise was '. . . my students do not prepare their text in advance, as they should. They are required to be able to define a number of specialised terms in economics, sociology, etc. I have been using the "Word sets" exercise with success . . . In addition to the specialised terms I also ask them to write down any new words. The exercise solves part of the preparation problem and the students also seem to learn more new words. Yours sincerely, Nicole Usigil.'

Acknowledgement

We got the idea from John Morgan, co-author of *Vocabulary*.

4.7 Picking your words

Tell the class a story you enjoy telling. Tell it, don't read it. It doesn't matter if you are not a native speaker – still tell it. You will get a strong contact with the listeners that way.

Tell the story again and this time ask the students to jot down 10–15 words that seem important to them in the story.

Invite them to compare their words in small groups.

Variation

A further dictation exercise that works well after a story-telling is to read the group 10–12 questions you have written that are connected with the story. They should be a lot more wide-ranging than traditional comprehension questions. Nobody writes anything during your first reading of the questions. You then read again, more slowly, and the students write down the three that interest them most.

The group gets up and moves around. Students put the questions that they have taken down about the story to other members of the group.

Note

For examples of wide-ranging questions about a story, see 'Revenge Questions' in *Once Upon a Time* by John Morgan and Mario Rinvolucri.

5 Thinking about meaning

Have a look at this sentence:

She made her dress.

On first reading did you take *dress* to be a noun or a verb? It can be either. Language is shot full with ambiguities, and this section invites students to play with meanings and make judgements about what things mean and if they mean anything.

You will find an exercise that does this at word level, 'Associations' (below). Others work at sentence level. In 'Does it mean anything?' (page 45) for example, students are asked to classify sentences into three categories: meaningful, 'iffy' and meaningless. An example of a sentence proposed is: *Potatoes move around searching for food.*

It is interesting that we rarely ask students to make judgements about meaning, and yet this is usually more relevant to their needs and therefore more interesting to them than the intricacies of grammar or the sound system. Most students find the semantic area one in which, even as learners, they have the right to make such judgements. Encouraging them to do this increases their confidence and the feeling that they are allowed to 'handle' the foreign tongue.

5.1 Associations

Dictate these words to your students and after each word leave them time to write down the first three associated words that come to their minds (don't indicate that the words have more than one meaning):

our/hour	urn/earn	Finn/fin
manual	dear/deer	lay
wood/would	sea/see	stable
seam/seem	bear/bare	bee/be
hold	Turkey/turkey	fur/fir
foul/fowl	wing	nose/knows/noes

Ask students to compare with each other the way they have spelt the words, the meanings they have attached to them and their associations. Now hand out photocopies of the lists below so that everybody is aware that the words as dictated have two or more meanings, connected by association with the words listed.

Two people who did the exercise came up with these lists:

PERSON A
our dog, house, holiday
manual hand, tiring, strong
wood dark, trees, chair
seem like, different, pretend
hold ship, crane, harbour
foul stink, old, rotten
urn Grecian, water, wine
dear wife, expensive, Sir
sea water, ocean, tide
bear brown, honey, Polar
Turkey Kemal Pasha, Anatolia, Kurds
wing palace, room, big
Finn sauna, forest, snow
lay priest, expert, ignorant
stable neurotic, reliable, firm
bee buzz, honey, sting
fur cat, fleas, coat
nose wine, handkerchief, red

PERSON B
hour glass, minute, clock
manual class, car, instructions
would like, modal, you
seam sew, blouse, trousers
hold baby, tight, cuddle
fowl hen, fly, egg
earn employer, low, money
deer stag, antlers, brown
see blind, glasses, clear
bare arse, arm, landscape
turkey Thanksgiving, USA, gobble-gobble
wing plane, bird, crash
fin fish, wet, foot
lay table, girl, egg
stable manure, hay, horse
be off, good, being
fir Wales, cone, mast
noes yeses, rejection, child

© Cambridge University Press 1988

5.2 Does it mean anything?

Ask the students to rule their pages into three vertical columns with these headings:

Meaningful | 'Iffy' | Meaningless

Give them a sentence, e.g. *Yesterday is tomorrow.* Ask them if they find it meaningful, perhaps meaningful ('iffy'), or meaningless. There may be different opinions.

Dictate these sentences and ask the students to write them in what they feel to be the appropriate column. The set of sentences is suitable for intermediate groups, though you may have to pre-teach some of the words:

45

Jamaica is edible.
Potatoes move around searching for food.
Aunts are parents.
Corporals can be bribed.
Beefsteaks become human.
Priests wear clothes.
The black mare led the procession to the town hall.
Paris is a living creature.
Grain is grown to be wasted.
Ghosts are alive.
Flies carry briefcases.
Church spires attract lightning.
Cheese is a form of drying.
Timber warps easily.
Trees grow downwards.
My brother stretches invisibly into the distance.

© Cambridge University Press 1988

The discussion after this exercise will cover a lot of ground – from vocabulary to the meaning of fantasy, to the art of poetry.

5.3 Translating ambiguity

Write these sentences, which are suitable for advanced students, on an OHP transparency. Tell the group that you will flash the first sentence up for five seconds and that they then have 15 seconds to write down its translation into their mother tongue. Mask all but the first sentence.

The cat feels cold.
Did you say he's engaged?
He has no ties at all.
He put his foot down.
I only touched the glass.
They swam for Ireland.
You can't punish them too severely.
She told him where to get off.
Visiting relatives can be boring.
That's a dangerous medicine cupboard.
They need a proper bath.
Her mother made her dress.
Angela likes music more than her brother.
POLICE FOUND DRUNK IN SHOP WINDOW
We didn't go to the museum because it was raining.

Flash the second one, and so on. You should not warn the students that all the sentences have two or more meanings.

Ask the students to work in fours and compare their translations. If you are teaching a mixed nationality group ask them to compare the meanings they saw in the English sentences.

At the end of the group work bring the class together and run through the ambiguities so that people are not left in the dark. One way of doing this is simply to ask grammar questions. For example, in *Visiting relatives can be boring*, is *visiting* a noun or an adjective? In *Her mother made her dress*, is *dress* a noun or a verb? In *POLICE FOUND DRUNK IN SHOP WINDOW*, is *found* active or passive?

A second lesson? Here are some more sentences to select from:

Guests stood drinking in the moonlight.
There will be a meeting on bicycles in Room 42 at 3 p.m.
She won't marry anyone.
The landlord is really tight.
He was looking at the girl with the binoculars.
She loved Jimmy more than anyone else.
He pointed to a flower in the garden which was blossoming beautifully.
The police were ordered to stop drinking at midnight.
He gave her a ring last night.
He was questioned by the officer in a state of undress.
The postman delivered the baby.

Variation

You can organise this exercise the other way round and have the students translate ambiguous mother tongue sentences into English. For example:

Il est parti dans sa voiture. (two meanings)
Man ist was man isst. (when *spoken* this sentence has four possible renderings)

Acknowledgement

The sentences used here were gathered by Cynthia Beresford.

5.4 Quantifying sentences

Tell the students that you would like them to write a quantification after each sentence you dictate. For example, if the sentence dictated is, *She lives a long way from her work*, the student might write '20 minutes by car' or '35 miles'. The elements quantified could include space, time, area or any other measurable category. Students should work individually and in silence.

Here is a possible text:

He gets home late in the evening.
She gets up fairly early at the weekend.
They live in a large flat.
She is overweight.
He is shorter than average.
They both watch a lot of TV each week.
He spends a lot of time in the bathroom.
She is a very quick reader.
She has a long tour to do for her work in Africa.
He is a good marathon runner.
They are both rather angry people.

After the dictation, invite students to compare their judgements.

Variation 1

You may want to use this sort of exercise after teaching the group about the quaint weights and measures that still persist in parts of the English-speaking or English-influenced world.

Here is a possible set of sentences:

He takes very large size shoes.
She ran a very high temperature for two days – after that it returned to normal.
He's put on a lot of weight recently, which has meant buying new shirts.
They have a large garden.
Their living room is pretty long, though not that wide.
She decided to sun-bathe on the patio – it was really very warm.
The airliner was travelling unusually fast and well above a normal cruising height.
The meat she bought was a lot more than three people could eat at one sitting.

Variation 2

It is also quite exciting to use this style of dictation when teaching ESP. Students write your sentences down and in addition to a quantification state what machine or process they are thinking of. The sparseness of the sentences helps the students select specifications which fit into their speciality.

It's got a lot of power.
It's a very expensive piece of equipment.
It rotates slowly.
One part gets extremely hot.*
It's a small quantity to work with.
It often breaks down.

* One student's quantification for this sentence was 'car exhaust – 500°C'.

It's noisy.
It takes a large charge to start.
It's efficient.
It saves time.

Acknowledgement

We discovered this exercise type in *Transactions* by Gysa Jaoui and
Claude Gourdin. The text is in French.

5.5 Him or her?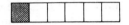

Give these incomplete sentences to one of the students and ask her to
dictate them to you at the board:

. . . was a very good boxer.
. . . wanted to be a ballerina.
. . . worked a lot in the garden.

Complete the sentences with *she* or *he*. Make it clear that you have a
choice over the third sentence – explain why you choose the sex marking
you do.

Now ask the students to take down the following sentences, adding in
she, *he*, *her*, *him*, *his* as they think appropriate, in place of *MmMm*.

MmMm drove a Mini.
MmMm was 80 and lived alone.
MmMm earned next to nothing.
They made MmMm study medicine.
MmMm went to visit MmMm in prison.
MmMm asked MmMm to wash a couple of things for MmMm.
MmMm father wanted to give MmMm a good start in life.
MmMm went to spend the weekend with MmMm mother.
MmMm hit MmMm children quite often.
MmMm took time off to look after the baby.
MmMm voted for the same party as MmMm at the elections.

Now ask students to explain how they chose the sex they did in each
sentence. It's best for them to work in small groups for this.

Notes

This is a particularly useful exercise for those students who confuse
she/he and *his/her*, as is sometimes the case with Spanish speakers, for
example.

The exercise also works well using names instead of pronouns.

6 Where on the page?

Most dictation involves a fairly straightforward conversion of the words that are read out into words on the page – the creation of normal continuous text. In this section the exercises are different. Students do not work their way neatly down the paper, but are asked to decide where on the page they need to place each utterance they transcribe. Having to choose the appropriate place on the page means that, in addition to having to listen carefully in order to interpret each message and relate it to those which went before, students also have to engage other parts of the brain which control and are affected by the eye and the hand.

For example, 'Words on a picture' (page 51) involves placing words on an illustration the students themselves have drawn. 'Import/export' (page 52) puts words on a world map. The notion of a map recurs in 'Handguns' (page 54). 'Around and about' (page 56) involves a scale of number, and 'Time dictation' (page 57) a scale of time – what is commonly known as a time line. And in 'Picture dictation' (page 56) we have a fairly common communication game in which students' comprehension is checked by their ability to reproduce on paper the spatial and descriptive information that has been dictated to them.

In normal use, language behaviour is generally accompanied by other activity involving the eye, the hand, the brain, etc. There is a lot to be said for reproducing this complexity in the learning situation. Dictation of any kind provides a nice blend of listening, writing, and checking through reading. This appeals to students whether they learn primarily in an auditory or visual or kinaesthetic way. These exercises, apart from introducing variety to the normal sequential writing process, motivate students by keeping them busy on several planes at once.

6.1   Words on a picture

This exercise is best done as a revision and deepening of known vocabulary.

Ask the students to take a piece of paper and draw a place where they were happy as children. Suggest that they draw a large picture using most of the paper in front of them. Make it clear that the worse they draw the better it is for the exercise. Explain that you are going to dictate the following words and ask them to write down the relevant ones on the appropriate places in their drawings. They take down only those words that fit.

Dictate some or all of these words:

comfortable	secure	light
warm	fashionable	noisy
away from others	imaginative	open
soft	late	under
bright	muddy	early
cosy	intimate	dangerous
old	ordered	blue
hidden	singled-out	cold
round	relaxed	forbidden
slippery	over-awed	with
folded	dreamy	out of sight
wet		clear
away		quiet
alone		smelly
exciting		hard to reach
dry		quick
high		new
delicate		dreams
oppressed		

Ask the students to add any other words of their own they want to.

Students work together in small groups and describe the place they have chosen and explain the placing of the words.

Acknowledgement

We learnt this exercise from Christine Frank, co-author of *Grammar in Action* and *Challenge to Think*.

Where on the page?

6.2 Import/export

Explain that English has a massive vocabulary, and that it is a hybrid language, a strong crossbreed rather than a delicate thoroughbred – it has taken words from many sources.

Give out enlarged photocopies of the outline map on page 53 to the students and have them study the examples. Ask the students to suggest a few loan-words from their first language which are used in English.

Now dictate the following words in twos and threes to provide a context. Students discuss where the words come from, then write them on the map as appropriate.

alcohol, assassin, zero, coffee (Arabic)
mother, father, brother (Anglo Saxon)
kitsch, doppelganger, kaput (German)
disco (French)
employee, divorcee, trainee (American English)
boss, hamburger, coleslaw (American English – two from Dutch, one from German)
skiing (Norwegian)
mosquito, potato, tobacco (South American Spanish)
tea (Chinese)
husband, want, get (Old Norse)
yacht, cruise, pickle (Dutch)
jazz, jukebox (West Africa via Black American English)
taboo, tattoo (Polynesian)
balcony, opera, umbrella (Italian)
telescope, telephone, atom (Greek)
shampoo, bungalow (Hindi)
sputnik, mammoth, robot (two from Russian, one from Czech)
whiskey, smithereens (Irish Gaelic)
pal (Romany)

© Cambridge University Press 1988

It is worth noticing how some words which originated in one language have found their way into English from another.

As a follow-up you can ask for words that have travelled from English into your students' languages.

Note

The following books provide useful reference for this exercise: *A Guidebook for Teaching about the English Language*, John Cormican and Gene Stanford; *A Dictionary of Foreign Words and Phrases*, Alan Bliss; *Words*, Victor Stevenson.

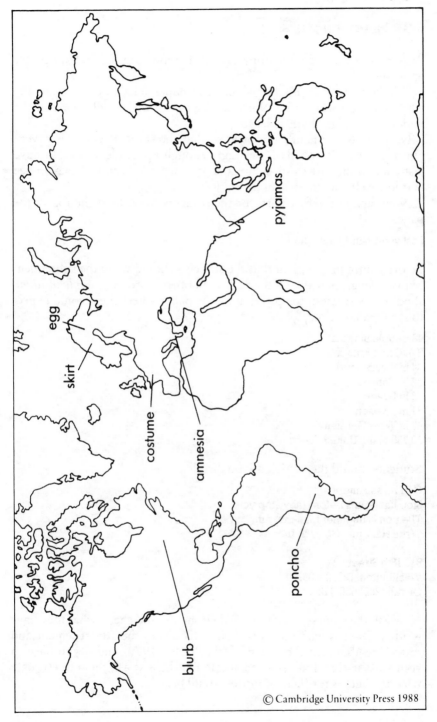

© Cambridge University Press 1988

6.3 Handguns

Prepare an enlarged photocopy or transparency of the handgun poster opposite.

Ask students to turn a largish piece of paper sideways and, using the whole of the sheet, write *North* at the top in the middle, *East* in the middle of the right-hand side, etc.

Now 'flash' the handgun poster so that the students get a very, very quick glimpse. If you flash fleetingly enough the students should have just enough interest to speculate and ask questions about a hazy image and so develop an interest in the subject.

Now dictate the first part, for the students to write at the top of the page.

Last year, handguns killed:

Before continuing explain that the students should write the subsequent phrases geographically on the paper. (In other words *48 people in Japan* should be written in the position on the paper where they would expect to see Japan on a map.)

48 people in Japan
8 in Great Britain
34 in Switzerland
52 in Canada
58 in Israel
21 in Sweden
42 in West Germany
10,728 in the United States

Students should then write, as you dictate:

God Bless America.
Stop handguns before they stop you.
The pen is mightier than the gun.
Write Handgun Control, Inc.
Now.
810 18th Street NW.,
Washington, DC. 20006.
Or call (202) 638-4723.

Now ask the students to compare their 'maps' and check what they have written. Discuss with students their reactions to the advertisement and to the credibility of the statistics (they're for 1979) and if you have in your class nationalities not represented in the text ask them to estimate what the figures for their countries would be.

Variation

We've found that many colleagues have their own variation of this exercise. Topics include house/room/office plans, parts of the body, clothing, cars, desktops, nuclear power stations, etc. The list is endless.

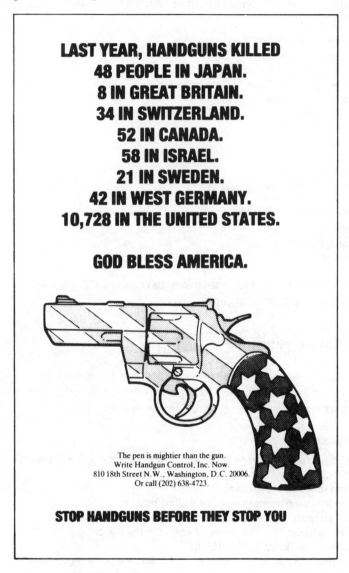

6.4 Around and about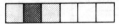

Have the students draw a vertical line down a piece of paper, numbered *nought* at the bottom and *a hundred* at the top. Dictate the following, explaining that the students should put each phrase on their scale as they feel is appropriate:

My grandmother's about 75.
She's in her mid-twenties.
She was born in the early sixties.
I'll buy a house when I'm in my late twenties.
In my early teens I was a hippie.
She's in her teens.
Mid-nineteenth century.
It's around half five.
Almost 40.
Just over the age limit.

© Cambridge University Press 1988

Now write a sentence about:
Your age.
Your date of birth.
Your future, etc.

Group the students and have them discuss each of the sentences (some of them provide options to argue about).

6.5 Picture dictation

Ask the students to take a sheet of paper and lay it lengthways. Check that they understand all the spatial terms in the dictation that follows. Dictate sentence by sentence – they *draw* what they hear.

The Quickest Way

Draw a line across your page from left to right – draw the line across the
    middle of the page.
Above the line there are waves.
In the top left-hand corner there is a sailing boat.
Draw a man lying on the sand in the bottom left-hand corner.
Top right-hand corner – there is a swimmer in the water.
The swimmer is shouting, 'Help! Help!'
Make a dotted line from the swimmer to the nearest point on the shore.
Draw a dotted line from the man on the sand to the swimmer.
What's the quickest way for the man on the beach to reach the swimmer?

Ask the students to work in pairs and answer the above question.

Note

You will find a sample picture and a suggested solution on page 115.

Acknowledgement

The visual problem was taken from 'Physics – where the action is', an article that appeared in the *New Scientist*.

6.6 Time dictation

Relax the students. A simple way of doing this is by getting them to breathe deeply and slowly. Or do the relaxation exercise outlined in 'Visualisation' (page 90). Or simply ask them to stand up and have a good stretch and yawn. Now guide the students through an image of the history of English. Speak in a calm, relaxed way. Pause frequently. Fill out the 'history' in any way you feel appropriate. The text below is a guide which you should feel free to amend. Ask them to try and visualise as much as possible. They may like to close their eyes. They don't have to write anything – simply listen.

The original Britons, Celtic sun worshippers, were conquered by the Romans and lived under Roman rule for 400 years. When the Romans left to defend Rome against the Barbarians no tradition of fighting was left and so mercenaries from North Germany were called in. Between about 449 and 485 more and more Jutes, Angles and Saxons settled here, either slaughtering or pushing the original Celtic population out into Wales, Cornwall and Brittany. So the basic Germanic grammar of English can be seen, and the similarity of the basic vocabulary to modern German – *eat, drink, cow, sheep, man, wife, house, sleep, weep.*

In 596 St Augustine was sent by the Pope to convert the local population. This conversion leads to the first small Latin influence on English vocabulary – *angel, priest, candle, master, school.*

From 737 onwards the Vikings began to invade and colonise – at one point they controlled the northern half of England. Although in the ninth century England became one political entity and the Vikings were effectively absorbed, as late as 1044 there was a Danish king of England. This influence is also reflected in the basic vocabulary of English – *want, dirt, egg, die, give, sister, sky.*

1066. The Normans invaded and conquered England. The Norman French at first formed the ruling class, but were later absorbed into the population. But the French had a large influence as they later intermingled and intermarried with the local population. Borrowings from French include – *veal, mutton, beef, crime, judge, tax, adolescence, royal, sumptuous, dream, amorous, commence.*

The next important influence is the Renaissance which led to a revived interest in classical texts. Borrowings from Greek include *democracy, encyclopaedia* and many medical terms; from Latin *expensive, education, capital, library, n.b., agenda, per annum, per capita, ad infinitum, etcetera.*

From the sixteenth century on, England was emerging as an imperial nation. As the British encountered other cultures they continued their habit of borrowing. Colonial borrowings from Hindi are – *dungarees, bangle, yoga.*

As the political and economic power of Britain has declined in the twentieth century, American power emerged. American English has influenced the language as it became an international language – *superstar, motel, ladies' room, senior citizen, memorial park.* English is still changing today, as is seen from the influence of British youth culture – *punk, new wave, splif*.*

Bring the students gently back to the present, centring them perhaps on an object in the room.

When you have finished talking, give out copies of the time line on page 59.

Now dictate the following word sets asking the students to write them down at the right place on the time line. (The criterion is when they first came into English, rather than their linguistic origin.)

superstar, motel
eat, drink, speak
veal, beef, mutton
cow, sheep
want, dirt, egg, die
education, encyclopaedia, expensive
church, angel, priest
splif, punk, new wave

Pause here for stocktaking. Have the students check their spelling and where they have put the words in time. When they have clarified their ideas continue with a second batch.

n.b., agenda, per annum, per capita
man, wife, meat, house
polaroid, blitz, ersatz
give, get, sister, sky
demand, amorous, commence
ladies' room, senior citizen, memorial park
crime, park, tax
candle, master, school
dungarees, bangle, yoga
adolescence, royal, sumptuous
sleep, dream, weep

---

* *splif* means 'hashish'.

Now focus the students on their own learning. What words do they think are lacking in English and should/will be borrowed in the future?

Some student suggestions we have collected are: one Norwegian student felt that English needed a word for day and night together – *døgn*, and for brothers and sisters – *søsken*; other students felt that *bricoler* 'fixing things as a hobby', *Waldsterben* 'dying forests', and *bio-computer* were needed; and a French student thought that *santé* sounded good in English.

Note

You will find a list of origins for the words in this exercise on page 115.

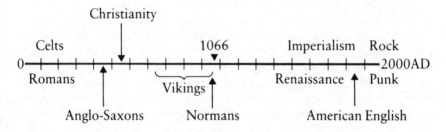

c

7 Text reconstruction

This section gives your students practice in writing with the assistance of a text that they have heard, either from you or from each other. Some of the exercises are quite traditional and straightforward, but our students have made it clear that they *like* them. Probably part of the attraction is the security of having some of the language provided, rather than having to tackle the problem of creating or reproducing a total text.

'Whistle gaps' (page 61) is like the common reading comprehension exercise in which students have to fill in gaps in the text in front of them. Here the gaps are in what they hear, and their contribution to the text has to be compatible with the surrounding language. In 'Words → dictation → story' (page 62) you provide words which students build into sentences before you provide a full story. Each level of text provision allows for reconstruction into larger text. The two 'cheating' exercises – 'Cheating dictation' (page 63) and 'Cheating with mime' (page 66) – consist of blanked-out texts for students to reconstruct. In 'Piecing it together' (page 68) all the text is available for reconstruction, but in random fragments. 'Dictogloss' (page 70) works at sentence level. You will find it an excellent way of helping more advanced students, through reconstruction, to get to grips with the style of a writer who is new to them. Finally, an exercise which involves quite a bit of preparation is 'Mutual dictation' (page 70). The effort is repaid by the amount of student cooperation which it stimulates.

This is not the only section where the students are given a degree of control over an exercise by being asked either to give the dictation or to provide language which you include in it. For other examples see 'Interference' (page 24), 'Adjectives' (page 76), 'Word by word' (page 77), 'Before and after' (page 77), 'Student story' (page 82), and other exercises in Section 8, 'The messenger and the scribe' (page 86), and some of the activities in Sections 9 and, especially, 11. There is a lot to be said for giving students the opportunity to do the reading themselves, or to provide text for it: the need to communicate accurately helps students to concentrate on what they are saying and how they are saying it; the need to convey emotion encourages them to alter their tone and pace and volume, to shout and to whisper – to use in English the range of expression that they are well used to employing in their own languages; and of course the spirit of cooperation is worth encouraging in itself.

Finally, it is valuable to develop the realisation by the students that language generated by them is at least as valid and interesting as text from the textbook or the teacher.

7.1 Whistle gaps

Many of us have done dictations in which we have given the students a written text with gaps in it. The students simply fill in the spaces as the teacher reads the passage. It is a way of making dictation that bit easier for the students.

Whistle gap dictation involves leaving gaps in the text you dictate, which in fact makes the task more challenging. Students have to think hard about the *meaning* of what they hear, and not just how to write it down. By increasing the difficulties involved in the task, the writing element becomes peripheral to the comprehension element, and there is plenty of evidence that peripheral learning of this kind – using language while the focus of attention is elsewhere – is a highly effective strategy. In this exercise you replace certain words with a whistle (or a clap or tap on the desk if you don't like whistling). Here is an example of a gapped text:

I'm walking (whistle) this street // in Leicester you see // late one afternoon // and (whistle) raining, // and suddenly there's this middle- (whistle) woman // blocking my (whistle), // standing in front (whistle) me // right in the (whistle) of the pavement. // And she looks at me with her (whistle) glaring, // and she (whistle): 'Why don't all you (whistle) bastards go home? You come here // and you take all the (whistle) and all the houses, // and all you (whistle) live on the Social.* // You've none of you // ever done a (whistle) day's work // in your lives. So go on, clear (whistle), // go back to the (whistle) // where you came from!'

(from *Soldier Soldier* by Tony Parker)

The missing words are listed on page 115.

Acknowledgement

We learnt this form of gapping from a workshop participant in St Gallen, Switzerland.

* Social Security benefits

7.2 Words → dictation → story

Put up these words on the board or OHP:

> win   hare   stupid   tortoise
> slow   ran   backwards and forwards
> challenged   race   proud   finishing post
> starting post   died   one day
> fast   home   boasting   seventy-four times

Ask a student to come to the board and circle two of the words – she then turns to the group and dictates a sentence that includes the two words. For example, having circled *stupid* and *home* she might dictate: *The stupid man went home.*

The rest of the students write down what she has dictated. If the dictating student makes a mistake the teacher waits until the others have written it down, then turns to the board and also takes it down. The teacher asks the dictating student to work on the sentence until she gets it right, on her own or with help from the group. The dictating student then designates another student to come to the board. This student circles another two words and dictates a sentence of his own containing them. Repeat this process with 10 to 15 people.

Now ask if anyone knows the story of the Hare and the Tortoise. Get people in small groups to reconstruct what they can remember of the story.

Tell the group one of the versions below, preferably the one that the students seem to know least (or you may know of or invent another version).

Acknowledgement

The central idea of the sentence dictation and its correction by the student with the help of classmates comes from the Silent Way, the approach created by Caleb Gattegno. The teacher acts as a neutral feedback mechanism, not the giver of solutions. The teacher merely triggers thought by the students about the language they themselves are using.

The Hare and the Tortoise (Aesop version)

Proud hare challenges slow tortoise to race.
They leave starting post.
Hare streaks ahead.
In sight of winning post hare lies down to sleep.
Tortoise plods past and reaches winning post.

The Hare and the Tortoise (Grimm version)

Hare boasts – tortoise challenges him to race.
Tortoise goes home to wife – asks how he can win.
She says: 'No problem'.
Mr Tortoise goes to starting post – she goes to near end of race course.
Hare streaks off and comes to Mrs Tortoise – very confused.
Runs back till he comes to Mr Tortoise – more confused.
Back and forth 74 times – dies of exhaustion.
Mr Tortoise wins.

7.3 Cheating dictation

The following text is suitable for advanced students. You can vary the
level of the exercise for a weaker group or weaker students by giving
them a grid with some of the words already filled in. Or you can make it
even more difficult by not reading the text through beforehand.

Read the following text to the students. Help them with any words
they don't know.

Toys of War

War is not a game. War is the pointless slaughter of people like you. Why teach
your children to play with death? Toy tanks, guns and rockets don't hurt, it's
true. And children like them too. But are they harmless?

A child can play at death and get up and have his tea; but weapons that don't
look much different from a toy shoot real bullets and kill real people. Do you
want to teach your child to solve problems by killing others? It's a dead-end
game. What possible fun can there be in pretending to kill a friend? Indeed,
what possible good can it be to kill anyone?

Boycott war toys. Buy creative toys. Buy toys for life not weapons of death.

(Issued by the Peace Pledge Union, 6 Endsleigh Street, London WC1)

Now hand out copies of the blanked text on page 65, one to each pair of
students. Their task is to reconstruct the passage you've just read. Give
them the following rules:

Text reconstruction

1 You will give them words from the text as and when you think they need them.
2 They can ask yes/no questions about the text. For example, 'Is the first word of the second paragraph "I"?'
3 You will answer only if the question is in correct English and only with a 'yes' or 'no'.
4 You, the teacher, can cheat – occasionally you will give them a word which is in the wrong place, or a word which is not in the text. But you will only do this when you offer a word unsolicited: make clear to the students that you will answer all questions and challenges accurately.
5 Students can challenge any word you give them.

Give the students a word for them to put into the blanked text and encourage them to fire questions at you. Do not cheat at first. Help the students by giving them words as necessary. As the text begins to fill out begin to cheat a little. You can quicken the pace by directing the students to specific points in the text as you offer them words, or you can slow the pace by cheating a little. Be crafty!

Variation

If your students like to be competitive, have a scoring system. Start the students off with a group score of 100. They get 1 point for an affirmative answer to a yes/no question, but lose 2 for a negative one. They gain 5 points for a correct challenge to a cheat, but lose 10 for an incorrect one.

Acknowledgement

This game was suggested by a computer program, *Quartext*, by John Higgins and Michael Johnson. In the program the students and the computer offer words alternately with a scoring system. The computer sometimes cheats. Our exercise is an example of reclaiming good ideas from the computer for the classroom. When the computer program is replaced by the teacher, the result is a more subtle, human game with greater group participation.

Toys of War

___ __ ___ _ ___. ___ __ ___ _____

_____ __ _____. ____ ___. ___ _____

____ _____ __ ____ ____ _____?

___ _____, ____ ___ _____ ___ _ _____,

__ _ ____. ___ _____ ___ ____ ___. ___

___ ____ _____?

_ ____ ___ ___ __ _____ ___ ___ __

___ ____ ___ ___; ___ _____ ____ ___ _

____ ____ _____ ____ _ ___ _____ ____

_____ ___ ____ ____ _____. __ ___ ___

__ _____ ____ ____ ___ __ _____ _____ __

_____ _____? __'_ _ ____ - ___ ____.

____ _____ ____ ___ ___ ____ __ __

_____ __ ___ _ _____? _____,

____ _____ ____ ___ __ __ __ _____

_____?

_____ ___ ___. ___ _____ ____.

___ ____ ___ ____ ___ _____ __ _____.

(Issued by the Peace Pledge Union, 6 Endsleigh Street, London WC1)

7.4 Cheating with mime

Have a copy of a text which lends itself to mime – the example below is for an elementary class.

Group the students, standing up, in a tight circle. Read through the text at normal speed. It is not important at this stage for the students to understand everything – the initial read through is just to focus attention on the text.

Now read the text a second time line by line. After each line pause and elicit an 'action' from the students. If the line is 'open the can' then the students should mime opening a can, etc. Students should show with

---

THE COKE MACHINE ROUND THE CORNER

You're standing in front of the Coke machine.

Put your hand into your back pocket.

Take out three 10p coins.

Put them in one by one.

You hear the machine click.

Choose your drink and press the button.

You hear a terrible groan from the constipated machine.

Clunk! A can drops down.

Pick it up.

Open the can.

It squirts Coke in your face.

Take a Kleenex out of your breast pocket.

Rub your eye.

Lick your lips.

Take a sip.

Burp!

© Cambridge University Press 1988

their bodies that they have understood you. Help with a little mime yourself if the students get stuck. (Props such as an empty Coke can and some 10p pieces are useful.) All the students should mime each action. It's unfair to the extrovert students to centre all the attention on them because others are not participating.

Read through a third time quickly again with all the students miming. Repeat again, this time at a breathless pace. Have fun!

Finally, pair the students and have them sit down with a copy between each pair of the blanked text below. Explain the rules of the cheating dictation (page 63). Give them their first word and wait for a question.

THE COKE MACHINE ROUND THE CORNER

___ __ _____ __ _____ __ ___

____ _____.

___ ____ ____ ____ ____ ____ _____.

____ ___ _____ 10p _____.

___ ____ __ ___ __ ___.

___ ____ ___ _____ _____.

_____ ____ _____ ___ _____ ___ _____.

___ ____ _ _____ _____ ____ ___

_____ _____.

_____! _ ___ _____ ____.

____ __ __.

____ ___ ___.

__ _____ ____ __ ____ ____.

____ _ _____ ___ __ ____ _____

_____.

___ ____ ___.

____ ____ ___.

____ _ ___.

____!

7.5 Piecing it together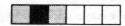

You are going to read a story for which the students know the text – but what they have is scrambled. First, read the story at a natural speed a couple of times. Then give out the sheet of phrases opposite. Give the students time to study it. Now ask them to turn the sheet over and listen to you reading the story a third time. Finally, the students use the phrases to reconstruct the whole text in their own writing:

I don't remember who the actress was but anyway she went into a restaurant and ordered a cake.
When the waiter brought the cake she said: 'I'd prefer a brandy – take the cake away, please.'
The brandy arrived. She drank it and then got up, as if to leave.
'Madam, Madam, your brandy,' the waiter called.
'What about it?'
'You've forgotten to pay for your brandy, Madam.'
'Nonsense, I got the brandy in exchange for the cake.'
'Well then,' said the waiter, 'you must pay for the cake.'
'Why?' she asked, 'I never ate it.'

Variation

Have the students in pairs cut up the sheet and sequence the phrases.

Acknowledgement

We learnt this idea from a colleague in a 1985 workshop in Eeklo, Belgium.

When the waiter brought the cake

and ordered a cake.

the waiter called.

for the cake."

The brandy arrived.

"Madam, Madam, your brandy,"

She drank it

I don't remember who the actress was

to pay for   "You've forgotten

she said: "I'd prefer a brandy

as if to leave.

"you must pay for the cake."

"Why?"   she asked,

and then got up,

but anyway she went into a restaurant

"Well then," said the waiter,

"What about it?"

"I never ate it."

your brandy, Madam."

– take the cake away, please."

"Nonsense, I got the brandy in exchange

Text reconstruction

7.6 Dictogloss

Choose a fairly long sentence that is not too difficult relative to the language level of the group. Here is one for a fairly advanced level:

We will no longer accept your doctor's statement as proof of unfitness for work, as we feel that if you are able to go to the doctor's you are able to come to work.

Tell your students that you will read them the sentence once *and once only*, after which they are to jot down the main key words they can recall and set about trying to reconstruct the sentence in writing as accurately as they can. Read them the sentence.

The first time you do this exercise you may have to relent and allow them a second reading, as people rarely pay attention until they discover that they need to pay attention first time round.

As they work at their rebuilding of the sentence, suggest that they get together in pairs and then fours.

Finally ask a 'secretary' to come out to the board to write up a final version. The secretary does not bring her script, but depends on suggestions from the group.

Students compare their corporate board version with your original.

Acknowledgement

This classic exercise was written up in *The English Language Teaching Journal* in 1963. In the late seventies it became popular in Australia. It is more fully described than here in *Once Upon a Time*, by John Morgan and Mario Rinvolucri. See also the article by Terry Tomscha in *Practical English Teaching*

7.7 Mutual dictation

This exercise involves students in combining two-part texts into one continuous piece.

Prepare copies of gapped text A and gapped text B opposite.

Sit the students facing each other in pairs. (In a traditional classroom have the front row turn round and face the second row, etc.) Give person A in each pair a version A sheet and person B a version B sheet.

Tell the students each has half the text. They should try not to look at each other's sheets. A dictates and B writes, then B dictates and A writes, and so on until the story is complete.

Finally have the students show each other their sheets to check for accuracy.

Text A

It was a _ _ _ _ _ _ _ _ _ _ and the bus was _ _ _ _ _ _ _ _ _ _ _.
There was a tall, handsome man standing _ _ _ _ _ _ _ _ _ _ _ _
_ _ _ _ _ _ _ _. Sitting _ _ _ _ him there was a _ _ _ _ _ _ _ _ _
_ _ _ _. The _ _ _ still _ _ _ a long _ _ _ _ _ _ _ to do. He _ _ _ _ _ _
talking to the _ _ _ _ _. He tells _ _ _ that he is very wealthy. _ _ _
pricks _ _ _ _ _ _ _ up. He talks to her _ _ _ _ _ _ _ _ _ _ _
_ _ _ _ – she looks at him _ _ _ _ _ _ _ _ _ _ _ _ _ _ _. _ _
tells her _ _ _ _ _ _ _ _ _ _ _ and _ _ _ _ _ _. She _ _ _ _ _ _ _ _
him with tender _ _ _ _ _ _ _ _. Finally he tells her he _ _ _ _ _
a _ _ _ _.

   The man says: ' _ _ _ ' _ _ _ _ _ _ _ the bus at _ _ _ _ _ _ _
_ _ _ _ _ – then we _ _ _ _ _ _ _.' _ _ _ _ _ _ _ up and gets _ _ _ the bus.
_ _ _ does not _ _ _ _ _ _ _ _ _ _ _ _ _. _ _ has taken _ _ _ _ _ _ _

Text B

_ _ _ _ _ _ very hot day _ _ _ _ _ _ _ _ _. _ _ _ very crowded.
_ _ _ _ _ _ _ _ _ _ _ _ _, _ _ _ _ _ _ _ _ _ _ _ _ _ _ _ _ _ _ _
near the front of the bus. _ _ _ _ _ _ _ _ near _ _ _ _ _ _ _ _ _ _ _
_ beautiful girl. _ _ _ man _ _ _ _ _ _ had _ _ _ _ _ journey _ _ _ _.
_ _ begins _ _ _ _ _ _ _ _ _ _ _ _ girl. _ _ _ _ _ _ _ _ her _ _ _ _ _ _
_ _ _ _ _ _ _ _ _ _ _ _ _. She _ _ _ _ _ _ _ her ears _ _. _ _
_ _ _ _ _ _ _ _ _ _ about his big farm – _ _ _ _ _ _ _ _ _ _ _ _ _ _
with real interest. He _ _ _ _ _ _ _ _ _ that he is sad _ _ _ lonely.
_ _ _ looks at _ _ _ _ _ _ _ _ _ _ _ _ _ sympathy. _ _ _ _ _ _ _ _ _ _
_ _ _ _ _ _ _ _ _ _ needs _ wife.

   _ _ _ _ _ _ _ _ _ _: 'Let's get off _ _ _ _ _ _ _ _ the next
stop – _ _ _ _ _ _ can talk.' She gets _ _ _ _ _ _ _ _ _ off _ _ _ _ _ _.
She _ _ _ _ _ _ _ look behind her. He _ _ _ _ _ _ _ _ her seat!

Text reconstruction

Complete version

It was a very hot day and the bus was very crowded. There was a tall, handsome man standing near the front of the bus. Sitting near him there was a beautiful girl. The man still had a long journey to do. He begins talking to the girl. He tells her that he is very wealthy. She pricks her ears up. He talks to her about his big farm – she looks at him with real interest. He tells her that he is sad and lonely. She looks at him with tender sympathy. Finally he tells her he needs a wife.

The man says: 'Let's get off the bus at the next stop – then we can talk.' She gets up and gets off the bus. She does not look behind her. He has taken her seat!

Variation 1

In language classes one is rarely asked to shout or whisper. People do pronunciation work without really exploring the expressive potential of the voice. In both shouting and whispering you experience a foreign language differently. In mutual dictation you can use both these modes. It is not only valuable but adds fun.

Ask the students to sit *across* the room from their partners – put on some low music for them to talk over. When you have given out versions A and B of the passage slowly raise the volume of the music so that people have gradually to raise their voices. Maybe you should warn colleagues teaching either side of you that this lesson will be a noisy one!

When the students have shouted the first paragraph of the story to their partners across the room, ask them to move close to each other and continue the mutual dictation, but *sotto voce*, in whispers. Make sure they still sit facing each other, or the temptation to look at the other's text will be overwhelming.

Here is another text, should you wish to try out the shouting and whispering modes of mutual dictation.

Spoons (complete version)

John died and went straight to Hell. Great long tables. Bowls of delicious food. John was amazed by this sight. Even more amazing were the spoons that lay beside the bowls. They were a full metre and a half long. When you tried to eat with them you couldn't get them into your mouth. So everybody in Hell sat looking at the delicious food and starving.

John asked if he could go up and have a look at Heaven. Up he went. Again great long tables laid with delicious food. Again great long spoons. He asked someone what the difference between Heaven and Hell was. The answer he got was very clear: 'In Heaven we use the spoons to feed each other!'

© Cambridge University Press 1988

Version A

____ ____ and went straight __ ____. Great long _____.
Bowls of _____ food. John was _____ by this _____.
____ ____ amazing were the__ ___ ___ ____ lay beside ___
_____ . They ____ _ ____ _____ and a half ____.
____ ___ tried to ___ ____ ____ you couldn't ___
____ ____ your mouth. __ _____ __ Hell sat looking
at ___ _____ ____ and starving.
    John _____ __ he could go up ___ ____ _ ____ at Heaven.
__ __ went. Again great long tables ____ ____ _____
____. ____ ____ long spoons. __ _____ _____
what the difference _____ _____ and Hell was. The
_____ __ ___ was very _____ : 'In _____ we use the
_____ to feed each ____!'

Version B

John died ___ ____ _____ to Hell. _____ ____
tables. _____ __ delicious ____. ____ ___ amazed __
____ sight. Even more _____ ____ ___ spoons that
___ _____ the bowls. ____ were a full metre ___ _ ____
long. When you _____ __ eat with them ___ _____'_ get
them into ____ _____. So everybody in ____ ___
_____ __ the delicious food ___ _____.
    ____ asked if __ _____ __ __ and have a look __
_____. Up he ____. ____ _____ ____ _____
laid with delicious food. Again great ____ _____. He asked
someone ____ ___ _____ between Heaven ___
____ ___. The answer he got ___ ____ clear: '__ Heaven
__ ___ ___ spoons __ ____ ____ other!'

Text reconstruction

Variation 2

By manipulating the gaps you create, you can use mutual dictations very successfully in mixed-ability groups. In the text given above, the gapping is roughly equally balanced. Student A and student B have much the same amount of writing to do. But if you know that A is a lot weaker than B, she should have less writing to do and should have a more complete text. B's text should have correspondingly fewer words in it. The beauty of this is that A, the weaker student, does more dictating than B and has a clearer initial idea of the whole passage than B. The weaker student is put in the position of being one up, though within a collaborative frame.

Note

Incidentally, if you are thinking of investing in a word processor, the preparation of this kind of exercise might be one reason for going ahead!

Acknowledgement

We first met this technique in a colleague group at the Bell School in Bath. We heard the bus story from a Syrian male colleague.

8 Using the students' text

At an elementary level students already have enough vocabulary to create a diversity of texts. But students themselves are not always aware of this, and you may have to find ways of encouraging them to notice the breadth and depth of their knowledge – see for example 'Adjectives' (page 76). All the exercises in this section involve eliciting a short text from students before dictating it back to them in some form or other. The values of drawing on student language have already been discussed (see Section 7).

Of the exercises in this section, 'Adjectives' (page 76) collects single words. In 'Word by word' (page 77) sentences are created, as they are in a different way in 'Before and after' (page 77). Sentences are the starting point in 'What have I done?' (page 79) and 'Opinion poll' (page 80) while 'Half the story' (page 81) and 'Student story' (page 82) depend, as you would anticipate, on the elicitation of more extended text.

When you realise how easy it is to get text from the group, it makes you wonder why so many hard-working people spend so many thousands of hours elaborating text sequences which have nothing directly to do with any given learner group. Textbooks? Home-baked bread often tastes better than the pre-packaged variety.

8.1 Adjectives ▨▨▨▨▨

Ask the students to shout out any adjectives that they know in English. Turn your back to them and write the adjectives on the board. Avoid turning round, prompting or encouraging. Be a neutral scribe. The following boardfull came from an elementary class:

---

single   traditional
        disgusting   warm
    delicious   shiny   modern   wet
  shy   boring   excellent   difficult   lucky
        cheap   international   married
                    popular
    excited   nasty   windy   fresh   pretty
        busy
    slow   strong   white   pink   lonely
  new   straight   exact   ridiculous
                sad   dry
    slim   easy   calm   expensive

When the group has dried up ask each student to select and write down the four most useful ones, the four most difficult ones and the four that she likes most. Pair the students and ask them to dictate their lists to each other. But the student taking down the words must take down the opposite* of the word dictated.

When the pairs have finished their dictations go back to the board and go through what they've produced.

This exercise is a valuable cue for a discussion of how many words your students need, how many words they know and use in their first language, how important vocabulary is, and how they can manage to function when they don't know a particular word. Equally, discussion of adjective endings comes in naturally here.

---

* Many opposites will be possible. For example, *international* from the list above might provoke *national, local, simple*. What opposite would you provide for *pink*?

Note

The examples above come from an unexceptional elementary group. At the end of a lesson the students were very excited to realise that they knew over 130 adjectives. If they had been asked beforehand how many adjectives they knew they would have wildly underestimated

8.2   Word by word

Divide the class into groups of about five or six. Give each group a large sheet of paper. The groups should not be able to see each other's sheets of paper.

Ask group A to write down the first word of a sentence. They dictate their word to the other groups. Group B proposes and writes down a second word, which they dictate to the others. Group C provides a third word, etc. until between them the groups have produced a 12-word sentence.

If one of the groups suspect that the other has proposed a word that has no possible follow-on in terms of sentence building, they may challenge: 'What would follow that word?' If the other group cannot give an adequate answer they can reject the word.

Variation

The exercise can equally well be done with pairs playing pairs or individuals playing individuals. It's best to have players sitting opposite each other rather than side by side, as this emphasises the game aspect. In a large class the teacher has to be everywhere at once, helping with doubtful sentences.

Acknowledgement

We learnt this exercise from John Morgan, co-author of *The Q Book*.

8.3   Before and after

Ask each student to write (*a*) a nice word, (*b*) a new (recently learnt) word, and (*c*) a 'grammar' word. When they have all three, write all their suggestions on the board/OHP.

⟫→

An elementary class came up with the following:

> **Nice words**: hard-work, lovely, fresh, woman, possible, exact, pretty, shut-up, mad, umbrella, marvellous, handkerchief, butterfly, happy.
>
> **New words**: hook, ugly, food, immediately, properly, needle, daffodil, fantastic, bendy, shadow, tangerine, bubbly, traditional.
>
> **Grammar words**: make/do, across, to be, why, would, to have, to find, to want, if, must, against, say, really, he/she, when, must, it is, they.

The teacher added *a* and *the*.

Before continuing check there is enough language in the grammar section. At a more elementary level there usually is but you might like to supply, say, *a*, *the*, *to be*, *to have*, etc. if the students haven't come up with them. At an intermediate or advanced level the students are liable to come up with less basic grammar words so a fourth category such as 'one of the most common words in the English language' is necessary to provide the 'guts' to facilitate sentence construction.

Now ask the students to make as many short sentences as they can from the words in, say, six minutes. They should use only the words written on the board. Ask them to write on slips of paper. Collect in their sentences.

Now ask the students to choose a partner and sit facing their partner. Tell each student to turn a piece of paper lengthways and to divide it into three columns. The first column should be labelled 'before' and the third column 'after'; the middle column is where they will take down the dictation. Explain that you are going to dictate some of their sentences back to them, they are to write them in the centre column, and then to add one, two, three or four words *either* before *or* after each sentence, any words – not just the ones on the board. Ask each pair of students to decide which one of them is going to add words *before* the dictated sentences, and which one *after*.

Choose and dictate the sentences you take a fancy to as you skim read the students' work. Dictate amended sentences – you correct any mistakes as you go along. Short pithy sentences work best. Give the students time after dictating each sentence to think up their additions. The 'before' students should *not* consult with the 'afters' at this stage.

When you feel you have dictated enough sentences ask the pairs to decide which of their sentences are meaningful across all three columns. Finally ask each pair to read out their best three-part sentence.

When the students from the example group had combined their 'befores' and 'afters' with the dictated sentences, some of their sentences read as follows:

BEFORE	DICTATED SENTENCES	AFTER
English people	wanted hard work	years ago.
He asks me	why is she pretty	because she likes herself.
Is it true	an ugly tangerine must be bubbly	to be perfect.
All teachers say	they want hard work	this afternoon!
Each day I ask myself	why is she pretty	because she likes herself.
When you move to the future	an umbrella is traditional	isn't it?
Look on the flower	it's a fantastic butterfly to find	on my birthday.
I don't know	why is she pretty	at this time.
Everyone's busy	they want hard work	in school.
In England	a woman wanted to be mad	yesterday.
In England	a woman wanted to be mad	after the dance.
In the family	an ugly tangerine must be bubbly	in the rubbish.
In my country	an umbrella is traditional	because rain never ends.
I know	a woman wanted to be mad	because she always dreams.
If it's true	it's a fantastic butterfly to find	in the city centre.

8.4 What have I done?

Offer the students some examples of skills you have acquired or experiences you have had. Among sentences we have used are these (notice the use of the present perfect):

I have learned to speak my mother tongue.
I've had two best friends.
I have learned to ride a bike.
I have spent some time in hospital.

Now ask each student to write down on a sheet of paper four experiences of their own.

Take in their sheets and then use individual experiences to make statements like this:

Maybe
Perhaps ... % of us have ... (+ individual's experience)
Probably

You may need to reformulate what the students have written in terms of language accuracy.

As the students take down the sentences you dictate, they supply their own guess at the percentage of the group who have had each experience. After the dictation get the students to read out their estimates. Finally ask those who have had the experience to put their hands up, and compare it with the estimates.

8.5   Opinion poll

Ask each student to take a piece of paper and write five sentences giving an opinion, each to include the word *home*.

Collect in these opinion sheets.

Ask the students to put a piece of paper lengthways and to make five columns with these headings:

I agree	I disagree	Most people in my country would agree	X . . . in my family would disagree	Our teacher probably agrees

The students should choose a person they know well in their family for the X in column 4.

Explain that you will dictate a selection of the sentences they have just written. They are to write each opinion down in the appropriate column.

Since there may well be mistakes in the sentences you have in front of you, dictate them in a corrected form, *without* pointing this out. Dictate 10 to 15 opinions.

Now get the group up and milling about the room – ask students to compare their categorisations of opinions. Sometimes strong, felt conversations develop at this point. Encourage people to stay in English.

At the end of the discussion phase ask students who are not sure whether they wrote the dictation accurately to dictate the sentences they are unsure about back to you at the board. This allows them to check out their doubts.

Note

This exercise can be done with other emotive key words. Think for example of *thirsty, on time, sleep, light, AIDS*.

8.6 Half the story

This is an exercise in shared story construction.

Dictate the sentences below, and give the instructions in parentheses using a different tone of voice.

Giovanni

Giovanni was having a rather heated exchange with his history teacher. She was getting more and more upset. (Please write the first few lines of the conversation.)

When Giovanni got home he went into the kitchen and said hello to his Mum. (Please describe her.)

She called the family to table and they all sat down to eat. It didn't take long for Giovanni's Mum and Dad to start arguing. (Write their argument.)

Giovanni couldn't stand it any longer. He left the table and went upstairs, banging the dining-room door behind him. When he got into his room he shut the door and put on some music. (Draw the music.)

© Cambridge University Press 1988

Ask the students to read their stories to one another in pairs or small groups.

Note

A more detailed description of this collaborative story-telling technique is to be found in *Once Upon a Time*, by John Morgan and Mario Rinvolucri. The book also gives two other story outlines to be done this way.

Acknowledgement

The story above was suggested by a primary school teacher of Italian to Italian migrant children during a workshop in Chur, in Switzerland. For more primary school ideas on the teaching of Italian, see *Oggi che Facciamo*, by Richard and Marjorie Baudain.

Using the students' text

8.7 Student story ⬜⬛⬛⬜⬛⬜⬜⬜

In this exercise, you dictate students' stories back to them. As a warm-up, tell your class a story.

Good topics for stories are:

- the time you were hottest/coldest
- a frightening experience with an animal
- coincidences
- driving tests/lessons
- getting something new
- the time I caught the wrong train/bus, etc.

Give the students a minute or two to come up with their own story in the area you have chosen. Ask the students to volunteer their stories. Keep a careful mental note of each story you hear. While the students are telling their stories forget your role as a corrector and focus your best attention on the content and style for the retelling.

After half a dozen or so stories, ask the students to get a pencil and paper. Dictate the story/stories you like the best, suitably enriching the language. You may find it odd at first to dictate without a written text in front of you, but doing this increases the immediacy for the students. Take down the text yourself on an OHP transparency as you dictate – doing the same task as the students provides a model text for correction and may also make you feel closer to the students.

Acknowledgement

We acknowledge a debt to Bernard Dufeu's work on *psychodramaturgie linguistique*, in which student-produced text is enriched and reformulated by the teacher. More information on Bernard's work can be found in the February/March 1983 issue of *Le Français dans le Monde*.

9 Lost in thought

The communicative approach to language teaching has made the EFL classroom a place where you're always interacting with someone or other. But students, sometimes, benefit from pools of introspective calm; from working on their own. In using many of the exercises in this section, we have noticed students turning inwards and focusing with surprising concentration on seemingly very simple tasks. Doing an introverted task surrounded by other people that you know is a lot different from doing the same task in the solitude of your room. Studying in a library can feel more comfortable than studying at home, however hard the chair.

A peculiar feature of schools is their habit of chaining lively teenagers to their seats from early morning to lunchtime. Moving around the classroom releases much pent-up energy, and in several of the exercises in this section such movement is a purposeful part of the learning process.

Conversely, in the field of sports training, mental and physical relaxation prior to practice is now routine.* As a sports trainer you would lose your job if you were foolish enough to allow your athletes to start work in a state of tension. The last four activities in this section include components designed to integrate relaxation into normal language work and to open channels to more personal communication. Some results of this relaxation are:

– freeing the mind from previous concerns
– raising energy levels
– improving recall
– satisfying the needs of people intelligent enough not to want to 'work hard'
– reducing frictions within the group
– calming the teacher.

It is worth giving some attention to the value of music, since it is employed in several of the activities which follow, as the titles indicate.

* See *Sporting Body, Sporting Mind: an athlete's guide to mental training* by John Syer and Christopher Connolly.

MEMORY!

83

Probably none of us wants music as a universal wallpaper, but it is significant that technology has been exploited in order to give us music in the restaurant as we eat, and in the car as we drive, and in the stress-provoking street as we jog. It is not only the case that we *can* both listen to music and perform other physical and mental functions as we do so; it is also that we benefit from doing so, from the relaxation and distraction the music provides.

Music in the form of songs is often used in the language classroom. Songs are an excellent carrier of vocabulary and of rhythm. In this section, music is integrated with unsung text. In classical Suggestopedia as developed by Lozanov, Baroque music is specifically chosen to slow the rate of the heartbeat and to make students more susceptible to language. Here, for psychological reasons, we have felt it useful to offer a choice of music to the students, though interestingly we have found that students themselves do frequently opt for Baroque or perhaps Romantic music. They seem to confirm that Lozanov got it right.

Note

For further reading on the encouragement of relaxation in the classroom, see *Memory, Meaning and Method* by Earl Stevick. Also useful are the *SEAL* journals.*

9.1 Delayed transcription

Post copies of the text on the front wall of the classroom. Tell the students this is a transcription exercise. They come to the wall and read the first bit of the text. They go back to their places and write it down. They come back to the wall for a second read and then go back and write down what they can hold in their heads, etc. No pens at the wall. A text suitable for elementary students is given opposite.

When most people have finished the transcription, take the texts off the wall and give them out. Students check their transcription against the original.

What do you do while the students are busily engaged in this activity? One option is for you to sit quietly in a corner and take the time to observe the students at work. There is plenty to watch: the way they read, walk, look and write.

Another option is for you to wander round the room reading what is being written and making notes for future reference of difficulties students are experiencing.

* Available from SEAL, c/o Michael Lawlor, The Forge, Kemble, Nr Cirencester.

Poem

I can't remember when
I was inside my mother,
But now I am outside
I wish I was inside again,
I can think how safe and warm and secure it would be.

When I look around sometimes and see
Disease and hate and wars and violence
I feel like running away
Lying down
And going to sleep.
This is how I imagine it was like in the womb.

But if I think again,
I realise that the reason why you were born
Or ever in the womb,
Was to be born
And do something –
And to think of going back to the womb
Is just really avoiding the point.

(Elaine Clark from *Stepney Words I and II*)

A third option is to read the work being produced and point out to the student *where* there is a mistake without telling her *what* it is. You might simply say, 'Check this out on the wall.' If you do decide to correct in this way, focus on recent mistakes. If the student is currently working on the end of the text don't point out something wrong in the second line – it's light years back in her experience. Don't speak to the student the moment she gets back from the wall as she needs to write down what she has in her head first. It's a mistake to interrupt the reading-to-writing process.

We feel that while the third option assuages teacher guilt ('I must make myself useful') the first two options are more useful to the students. The third option can hinder student concentration and break into a sometimes fairly private learning world.

Acknowledgement

We learnt this idea from Jill Johnson.

9.2 The messenger and the scribe

Post copies of the text on the front wall of the classroom or out in the corridor. Here is an example:

The Wise Judge

This story took place in China.

A crowd of people gathered round an acrobat.

Suddenly a man who sold fried doughnuts shouted, 'My purse, where's my purse? Thief! Thief!'

The doughnut seller pointed to a man who sold hats and said, 'It's him – he's the thief.'

The hat seller said, 'No, no, I didn't take your coins.'

A judge was passing by that way and heard the two men shouting. He listened to both men and then said, 'Bring me a bowl of water.'

The judge took a coin from every woman and man in the crowd.

How did he find the thief?

© Cambridge University Press 1988

Pair the students off and designate one in each pair as the 'scribe' and the other as the 'messenger'. The messenger goes and reads from the wall, brings back as much as she can remember, and dictates it to the scribe.

Often in the course of the activity, a messenger will get fed up with her partner's slowness as scribe and grab the pen herself. If this happens have the scribe become the messenger. Encourage this role switch anyway about half way through the exercise.

Finally have your students work in groups and decide how the judge identified the thief. You will find a likely answer on page 116.

Variation 1

This activity can become a competitive one in which the pair to transcribe the passage on the wall fastest gets the highest marks.

First tell the students that accuracy is as important as speed. When the first pair finishes award them 50 points, with 48 to the next, 46 to the next, and so on. Do this on the board.

But tell the class that the competition is not yet over as they are going to correct each other's dictations, and all mistakes will be deducted from the arrival order score. The pairs exchange dictations, correct them by comparing them with the original passage that you give out, and deduct all mistakes from the score on the board. This gives the final score, and it may turn out that the winners are a slower pair who have been more accurate.

Variation 2

Divide the class into two groups. Each group should form a line with the text at one end and a student who has a pencil and paper at the other. The students relay the dictation along the line to their 'secretary' as in 'Chinese whispers'.

Acknowledgement

The story above is a traditional one told to us by Charles Wong.

9.3 Brief glimpses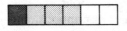

Prepare an OHP transparency with these words on it:

own	far away	died	sad
cold	lonely	damp	company
husband	tom cat	room	children

Prepare an OHP transparency with this text on it:

My cold old house

I live on my own,
In a cold damp room,
No one to talk to,
No one to see.

My children are married,
They live far away,
My husband died
On a cold winter's day.

I feel oh so lonely,
I feel oh so sad,
The only company I have is my tom cat,
He's a lovely little cat.

(Tina Balman from *Stepney Words I and II*)

If you have no OHP you can easily use your board for the words and prepare the text on strips of card.

Lost in thought

Tell the group that you are going to show them 12 important words from a text. You will let them see the words for only seven seconds. After viewing they are to jot down as many as they can remember. 'Flash' the words on the first transparency.

Flash the words up again, this time for five seconds. They try to complete the list.

Now let them have a good long look at the words. Explain any that they don't know.

Now show the second transparency, masking all but the first line of the text, and allow them to see it for five seconds. They write it.

Mask all but the second line of the text and flash it up for five seconds. Continue till they have got the whole text.

Students now exchange transcriptions, and you let them see the text for as long as they need to correct their neighbour's work.

Acknowledgement

The idea of flashing words at a group is used in *Vocabulary*, by John Morgan and Mario Rinvolucri, and originally derives from a seminar given by Alan Maley and Alan Duff.

9.4 The never-ending story

Ask the students to have pencil and paper on their desks ready for a dictation. Go to a far corner of the room (or outside into the corridor), ask the students to gather round, and then read the text once through to them:

A woman goes into a shop to buy some shoes – she chooses a pair for 12 dollars. She gave the assistant a 20 dollar bill. As the shop assistant had no change he went to a nearby restaurant to get some. He gave the customer 8 dollars change. A few moments later the restaurant owner came fuming into the shoe shop. 'That 20 dollar bill you just gave me is a forgery,' he shouted angrily. The shop assistant gave him a new, good, 20 dollar bill.

The problem is this: how much did the shoe shop lose on these transactions?

© Cambridge University Press 1988

When you have finished the first reading tell the students you will read the text a second, third, fourth, etc. time. They are to listen to as much as they can retain and then go and write it down. They can come back and forth as many times as they want. Loop back and begin reading again: *A woman goes into a shop to buy . . .*

Students should go and write as much of the first sentence as they can remember. You continue reading as the students gather round again having written their first sentence or part of a sentence. They should listen for another sentence to take back and take down (imprinting the words in their short-term memory). Everybody works at their own pace. You continue reading the third loop and a fourth and so on. A time will come when you can stop. (Reading the story through for the umpteenth time you may start going glassy – in a way you are practising self-hypnosis. Make an effort to continue reading with meaning.)

When early finishers have got the whole story down, get them to pair off with those who have not yet finished and work out a solution to the problem. If different groups reach different conclusions get them working together. Finally give out copies of the text so the students can check what they have written.

Variation 1

You could make three or four tape recordings of the story and bring three or four cassette players to class. Place the machines along the front wall. Students come out from their places and wind the machines forwards as they need. An advantage of the cassette recorders over the teacher's voice is that the students have more immediate control.

Variation 2

In the language lab, record the story onto all the student machines. Ask the students to sit *away from* the machines. They walk over to their machines to do the listening, going back to their chairs to do the writing.

Acknowledgement

This story is told in *A Handbook of Structured Experiences for Human Relations Training*, edited by J.W. Pfeiffer and J.E. Jones. It probably originates in North India, though the above title does not acknowledge a source.

Notes

You will find other problem stories in *Mind Matters*, by Alan Maley and Françoise Grellet, and *Towards the Creative Teaching of English*, edited by Lou Spaventa.

The solution to the problem is on page 115.

9.5 Talking to themselves

Do you remember how interesting it was to hear your own recorded voice for the first time? This technique capitalises on that interest.

In the language lab, you speak the first sentence of a text into the students' earphones, but not onto their tapes. Each student then starts her machine and repeats the sentence as accurately as she can onto her own tape. She stops her machine. You read the next sentence. She records it in her own voice, etc. In this way, the students build up a recording of themselves – not you – telling the story.

The students then take dictation from their *own* voices.

In this exercise students are working as much on their pronunciation and intonation skills as on their ability to re-encode English in a written form.

Acknowledgement

We first learnt the exercise from Judith Sluggett, who has taught Euro MPs in Strasbourg. It also features in *Bring the Lab Back to Life*, by Philip Ely.

9.6 Visualisation

This exercise involves no written response from the students, yet in some ways you are asking them to respond to your spoken words in a very comprehensive manner, showing not only their understanding of your text but also its total effect upon them.

Before doing the dictation you need to get the group fully relaxed. The relaxation exercise suggested here is one of many.

First ask the students to sit in their chairs in a physiologically comfortable position: feet flat on floor, hands flat on thighs, back straight against the chair back and head held upright. In this position the fewest muscles are tense. Arms folded might be psychologically comfortable, but not muscularly relaxed.

Tell them they may shut their eyes if they wish. Some students feel uncomfortable if forced to close their eyes.

Speak these lines to the group in a quiet, calm, but not soporific tone (leave longish gaps between the sentences):

I notice my left hand on my left leg;
I notice the contact between the hand and the leg.

I notice my left arm on my left thigh;
I notice the contact between them.

I move my attention to my left foot;
My left foot is on the ground.

I notice the contact between my left foot and the ground, through my shoe;
I notice how my left foot is firmly on the ground.

I move up my left leg and notice the way my left thigh rests on the chair;
There is contact between my left thigh and the chair seat.

Repeat the above for the right side of the body. Then continue:

I notice the contact between my back and the back of the chair.
I notice the weight of my body and the contact it has with the chair.
I realise my body is heavy on the chair.
But my head, my head is high above the chair.
My head is not heavy, my head is high and clear.

Leave a pause. Then tell the group you are going to read them a Japanese poem (see page 92) and ask them to just let it flow over them.

Now tell the group you will read the poem again, line by line, and ask them this time to picture the written form of the words as they hear them. Ask them to visualise each word as a shape in their minds. Where the lines are long, break them up into sub-sections and allow longish pauses after each bit you read, thus giving time for the visualisation to take place.

To finish off the exercise ask people to imagine what they will see when they open their eyes; the shapes, colours, textures and people they will see when they 'come back' into the room.

Finally ask them to gently open their eyes, look around and stretch. Have a stretch yourself.

People may want to talk about their experience through the relaxation and the listening. They may want to be alone with themselves. They may want to look at the text of the poem. (You could post it round the walls of the room.)

The beauty of this exercise is that you have no way of checking what the emotional and intellectual work the students are doing may be. Despite your powerful suggestions the students are free to be doing what they need to during this 'lesson'.

If this is the first time you have done a relaxation exercise with a group, some people may not manage to relax. It takes a bit of getting used to. If the group are in their teens you can expect a good bit of initial giggling and fun-poking. With people of this age it is worth pointing out that relaxation exercises are absolutely integral in high-level sports training, and in other types of physically demanding activity. Adults who have had maternity training or done yoga work will take to this kind of exercise with natural ease.

D

Dinner

Go out in a gust-thrashed downpour
like a drowned rat
buy three pints of rice
for 24 sen and 5 rin
five dried fish
one pickled radish
red ginger
eggs from the chicken coop
seaweed hard as beaten steel
fried dumplings
salted bonito guts

Heat some water
eat like hunger-devils: our dinner.

The storm builds
slams against the roof-tiles
shakes, rattles the house.
Our appetite holds out sturdily,
food turns into blood, urges instinct.
Soon, surfeited, blissful
we hold hands quietly
cry unlimited joy in our hearts
and pray:
may the daily trivia have life
may life's every detail be illuminated
may each of us overflow
may we always be full.

Our dinner acquires
a power fiercer than the storm.
Eating done, satiety
awakens in us a mysterious lust
makes us marvel at our limbs
and burn in the violent rain.

This is dinner for poor people like us.

(from *Chieko and other Poems of Takamura Kotaro*, translated by Hiroaki
Sato)

Acknowledgement

We first experienced the above described form of relaxation exercise in a
workshop led by Bernard Dufeu, one of the initiators of *psychodramaturgie linguistique* (see his article in the February/March edition of *Le
Français dans le Monde*).

9.7 Musical script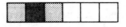

This exercise employs music to open up students to receive the language you dictate.

Give out your text* and ask the students to translate it into their own language. It is important that the students choose the variant of their language they feel most comfortable with. Explain clearly that they are to translate idiomatically, *not* literally – the purpose being to understand the English in relation to their own language. Walk round, checking their work but don't correct errors except glaring semantic ones. (Students do tend to make mistakes in their own language when they are translating from English, but this is not important here unless the translation shows that they have misunderstood the English.) If you teach multi-lingual groups English will be the normal working language. For this exercise group the students according to their mother tongue, but make sure they keep using English as the working language.

Students who have time can highlight or underline useful or interesting chunks from the text.

Now read the English text to music. The students should not write during this first reading. The music should be something relaxing. Baroque classical music or electronic music is suggested. If in doubt choose something you would find acceptable as background music when you are working, or ask the students what kind of music they like to work to. Make it clear to the students that they can choose whether to look at your text or their translation, or just listen to your voice and the music.

Read slowly, and with lots of pauses. Try to fit your voice and pace into the flow of the music. Keep the music loud, as loud as your voice. The relationship of your voice to the music is more important than reading in a naturalistic tone.

Now dictate the text to the students, still keeping the music loud – in opposition to your voice. Keep pace with the music, reading slowly with pauses, but make it clear that they can refer to the English text or their own translation. You will find that most students rarely refer to the text, preferring to check their performance afterwards.

Why does this work?

Students, notwithstanding the extreme artificiality of the format, see this as an extremely realistic task. There is usually background noise from jukeboxes, traffic, machinery or general hubbub when they are trying to listen to English, and the *loud* music mirrors this.

---

* This exercise is an ideal review activity. Write the dialogue to contain the structures and vocabulary which you have done in the previous few days. Make the language slightly easier than your idea of what the group knows, as the lesson is meant as a relaxing review, to fix concepts and aid memory. Do not introduce new material.

Many people listen to music when they work. It's relaxing and they find that it raises their energy levels and aids concentration. After doing this exercise for the first time it's worth asking which students listen to music when they are studying alone and inviting them to suggest music for the next dictation.

Students enjoy translation. If students are legitimately allowed to use their mother tongue productively once in a while, they will be less grumpy about being asked *not* to translate at other times.

The students should be able to comprehend the dialogue easily and without anxiety. The dialogue should be as bland as possible – students are often presented with 'authentic', 'funny', 'useful', etc. type dialogues, but sometimes a bland dialogue is refreshing both as a change and as a way to give students room to flesh out a dialogue using their own imagination. Here is an example. All the dialogue, including the scene setting and the names of speakers, should be read.

The Job

(Maria is having an interview with Margaret for a job as an au pair. They are sitting in a very posh living room in beautiful armchairs.)

MARGARET: Well now. Don't be nervous Maria. (Margaret looks very English, very snobbish and very over-dressed.) I just want to ask you a few questions.

MARIA: Mm-Mm. Yes?

MARGARET: Where do you study?

MARIA: At Eurocentres.

MARGARET: And how long are you staying in England?

MARIA: Until the middle of next year.

MARGARET: Right. Have you ever been an au pair before?

MARIA: No, but I've looked after my sister's children a lot since her divorce.

MARGARET: I see. Good. Can you drive? If you can drive you can take the children to school every morning.

MARIA: Yes. I've been driving for ages. I'm a very safe driver.

MARGARET: If you like you can borrow the car occasionally at weekends.

MARIA: Oh. That's nice. If you decide to take me how much will I get paid?

MARGARET: Well. You get a room, meals and I'll give you some pocket money. But you won't have to work for more than four to five hours a day. And it's light work. I'm sure you'll like the kids.

MARIA: That sounds fine. These chairs are nice and comfortable.

MARGARET: Yes. When you get cosy it's difficult to get up again.

Acknowledgement

This exercise is derived from Suggestopedia.

Note

The dialogue opposite was originally written to review units 7 and 10 of level 2 of the *Cambridge English Course*.

9.8 Musical conversation

Music is used again in this exercise, but this time the language dictated has come from the students themselves.

An important feature of Community Language Learning is that the students control the language and so produce their own text. Lessons with music, based on Lozanov's Suggestopedia, offer relaxed learning but depend on the teacher's text. This exercise combines the best of both worlds. (For more on this see Section 11.)

Choose suitable music to accompany a text like the one below (see the introduction to this section). Give out copies of a transcript of a group conversation from your own class. The transcript is to be used for reference by the students during the dictation as and when they wish. The following text is an example of a transcript that has been corrected. (The bits in *italic* are corrections.)

Read the text through once to the music, with long pauses for reflection. The second time dictate continuously, again to music (for variety you might like to use a different piece of music).

The students' own language slips effortlessly onto the paper without tension.

ISMAIL: What are you thinking about?
INES: This evening, I'm coming to school to see the play. Are you
            coming too?
JUAN: No, I'm not, because *I haven't got* a ticket.
ELIZABETH: I've got a ticket and *I'm going* tomorrow.
JUAN: Who are the actors? *Are they* students here?
INES: I think there is somebody *from the school* in the play.
ISMAIL: *What kind* of play is it?
INES: I'm not sure, but I *think* it's a musical.
ELIZABETH: No, it's not a musical, because the Italian girl *who lives with me*
            says, 'No, it's not a musical' because she is acting in the play.
ISMAIL: How much does a ticket cost?
ELIZABETH: 50p.
ANA ROSA: Is Paul going to the play? He said, 'No'.

Lost in thought

URSULA: Do you have any special decorations in your country for Christmas?

ANA ROSA: Yes.

URSULA: What?

ANA ROSA: It's *the same as* here.

JUAN: Spanish people *haven't got* a Father Christmas. Spanish people have got three kings.

MANUEL: Three magic kings.

ELIZABETH: In Brazil we have magic kings *too* and Father Christmas.

FLORENCE: *It's very stupid.*

JUAN: The magic *kings'* names are Melchior, Gaspar and Balthasar.

FLORENCE: It's *even more* stupid.

JUAN: Florence, *do you believe* in Father Christmas?

MANUEL: Yes, because you are stupid.

FLORENCE: Spanish people are very *annoying.*

MANUEL: *Really?*

FLORENCE: Yes, really.

MANUEL: Are you sure?

MANUEL: Rolf, why did you murder the postman?

BEATRIX: Manuel, which postman?

MANUEL: The Turkish postman.

ROLF: There *aren't* any Turkish postmen in England. Why are you asking me? *Do you hate* postmen?

MANUEL: Me?

ROLF: Yes, you.

MANUEL: Not me!

ROLF: Yes, you.

BEATRIX: Manuel, was your father *called* Salvador Dali?

ROLF: Where is Salvador Dali?

ASTRID: *Time to go home.*

9.9   DIY* words and music

Ask for three or four volunteers who would be interested in making a dictation tape. Ask them each to bring a personal tape of their favourite music (something without words) and a simple text of their own of less than ten sentences, that they think would be of interest to the rest of the group. Stress that the text is to be read aloud and so must be reasonably simple, and that the music should be relaxing.

Gather the volunteer students around two tape recorders. This is best done while the other students are doing an alternative activity. Have the students each record their text on the first recorder while the music they have selected is played as background on the second. Let them have complete control of the speed at which they read, the relative loudness of their voice to the music, and how they fit their voice to the music.

When each of the volunteers in the sub-group has made a recording of their text, ask them to choose a 'disc jockey'. Bring the class back together. The student DJ plays the whole tape through. The listeners select the text they would most like to take down. The student DJ then controls the tape recorder which dictates the text, helping the students as much as is necessary when difficulties occur, and checking the dictation for the class at the end. The DJ should also have a written copy of the texts.

This exercise works better with students who have worked with music in the group before, for example through the previous exercise 'Musical conversation' (page 95).

Variation 1

The recording work outlined in the second paragraph above can be done as homework.

Variation 2

If you have a small group and can scrounge enough tape recorders from your colleagues' classrooms, this exercise works well as group work with the whole class involved. In this case exchange tapes, texts and DJs across groups rather than bringing the whole class together.

* Do it yourself

10 Finding out about each other

Traditionally, dictation has been seen as an end in itself or as a revision activity. The text involved has come from outside – from a collection of passages or perhaps from the course text, and usually the act of dictating and transcribing has been separated from other activity and conducted as a compartmentalised and somewhat impersonal exercise. We hope that at least some of the tasks offered in earlier sections have shown that this need not be the case. Dictation *can* be integrated with other activities, and it *can* draw upon the personal language and experience of you the teacher and of your students.

The next section in this book will be looking at dictation in the context of Community Language Learning. In this section, we offer some dictation activities which engage the personalities and experience and emotions of you and your students, as material for the language which is transmitted.

Some of the activities which follow lead naturally to pair or group discussions. You have the opportunity to find out more about your students and vice versa. In 'The teacher's autobiography' (page 99), for example, the teacher dictates four sentences about her own life, only three of which are true. The students have to take down the one they think is false. The juice of this exercise lies in the discussion afterwards as students compare their impressions. The dictation itself provides a warm-up or incubation period during which ideas form and take shape in individual minds.

An essential feature of activities of this kind is that – as illustrated in previous sections – the learners are engaged in a double task: not only taking down the dictation, but making a personal judgement about what they have heard. The idea of offering students a double activity parallels normal experience. Very often people do things better when they have two things to pay attention to. Some like to listen to the radio as they cook, or watch television while ironing, or do mathematics with pop music swirling around them or drive while talking to a passenger. We have found the same with dictation: it is more enjoyable and is done with more energy when there is a parallel thinking task to accomplish. Many classroom hours are spent in states of very low energy and this section seeks to remedy that situation.

10.1   The teacher's autobiography

In this task, you are revealing to your students something of yourself.

Write batches of four statements about periods in your life. In each batch of four, three should be true and one should be false. You'll need about ten batches. One of us wrote the following examples:

I went to primary school.*
I didn't want to learn to read.
I began to love reading.
I loved reading history books.

At university I worked very hard.*
I studied Chinese as well as Spanish and French.
I rowed for two terms on the river.
I met my present wife at university.

My wife and I lived in Athens for three years.
I worked there as a journalist.
My daughter was born in Athens.
My wife and I both went mountain climbing in northern Greece.*

Tell the students they are going to hear sets of four statements. One of the statements in each set will be false. They are to write down only the statement they believe to be false.

Read each group of statements three times. Suggest that the students listen carefully for the first two times and only write during or after the third reading. Give a fourth reading if you are asked to.

After the selective dictation get the students working in small groups, comparing the sentences they picked out as false. Give them copies of the sets of statements and time to read them through.

Finally read out the false statements.

The examples we give above were used with a lower-intermediate group on only the fifth meeting with them. None of the students had sufficient information to pick out the false statements from prior knowledge. They simply had to work on feel, intuition and, in some cases, internal evidence within the sets of statements. The task would have been less challenging had the students known the teacher better.

Variation 1

A natural follow-up to the teacher autobiographical dictation is to ask students to prepare similar sets of statements which they then read/dictate to each other. In this way students explore one another's pasts.

* The statements marked * are false.

Variation 2

The versions proposed here are personalised as we feel it natural for teacher and students to find out a lot about each other over the span of a course. You could of course use the same technique as a kind of dictation quiz on more impersonal topics like history, botany or geography. For example:

Sydney is the capital of Australia.*
New Caledonia is the French territory nearest Australia.
Sydney is in New South Wales.
Canberra is a rather small town.

Acknowledgement

This exercise type was suggested by Gail Morare who works with the Adult Migrant Education Service in Melbourne, Australia.

10.2 About myself

Give the question page opposite to one of the students, and ask her to dictate any question she wishes to you. Take it down on the board and then answer it: the 'I' is you! Ask her to choose and dictate a second question. Write it somewhere else on the board and again answer it. And a third one.

Take back the page and dictate 10 to 15 of the questions, leaving time for the students to answer the questions with reference to themselves. The students write their questions and answers on completely blank sheets of paper (A4 is the minimum size suitable). Encourage them to write all over the paper, rather than from the top down.

Invite the students to discuss their answers in pairs.

Draw the group together again and ask them to dictate the questions back to you. You write them on the board. This will allow them to check spellings.

Variation

You could ask the students to each pick a person in their lives whom they know well. The questions would then need to be in the third person:

Who can she or he trust?
Where does she or he come from?

This variation brings a whole new wave of people into the classroom: significant others.

Acknowledgement

This set of questions was devised by Keith Jones as a worksheet to go with his video of *The Hermit*, to lead students into thinking about the hermit's character. You might like to try applying this technique to literary texts that you are familiar with.

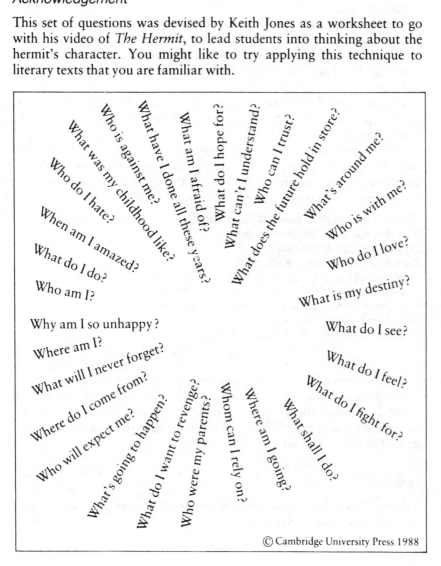

10.3   How can you say that?

This task explores the ways in which it is appropriate to talk to different people that we know. It develops a sensitivity to language in personal communication.

Ask the students to turn their writing sheets lengthways and produce a grid like the one opposite.

Say something to the group loudly. Then ask them *how* you spoke. If possible elicit *loudly* and have them write *loudly* at the top of the first column.

Repeat with these ways of speaking: softly, angrily, kindly, fast, clearly, politely, sexily, boringly, threateningly. Add *in a . . . way* as a further category.

Tell the students you are going to dictate questions to them about the way different people speak in given situations. They should take the questions down and answer by ticking the appropriate column or by writing the right word(s) in the 'in a . . . way' column.

How do I (the teacher) speak to this group?
How do policemen speak to teenagers?
How do you speak in a shop?
How do people speak to each other in church?
How does/did your father speak to you at the table?
How do you speak to your best friend on the phone?
How would God speak to you, if this could happen?
How do you speak to toddlers?
How does your favourite TV star speak on the screen?

© Cambridge University Press 1988

Tell students to add five more questions of their own to fill out this set.

Finally invite students to compare their answers and explain the contexts in which the speaking takes or has taken place. Finish the task by drawing together on the board the new adverbs students may have needed to use in their 'in a . . . way' column.

Note

More questionnaire dictations can be found in *The Q Book*, by John Morgan and Mario Rinvolucri.

HOW WAS IT SAID?		WHAT WAS SAID?
loudly		

10.4   Who can you say that to?

This task explores the topics (and emotions) you are likely to raise in conversation with others.

Tell the students to turn a piece of paper lengthways and to rule five columns. The column headings are:

For adults:

Stranger in a train | *My partner* | *My boss* | *My mother* |

Or if you have a class of teenagers:

My boy/girlfriend | *My mother* | *My best friend* | *My favourite "star"* |

Tell them to put a person of their own choice as the fifth column heading.

Write up on the board: *How much do you weigh?*

Ask the students who they feel they could say this to. If they could say it to a boy- or girlfriend, then they should write the question in that column. If they could also say it to their mother, they should tick the 'mother' column, and so on.

You then dictate the questions below, which they put into the column they feel makes most sense. They also tick other appropriate columns.

1 Do you love me?
2 How much money do you earn?
3 How old are you?
4 Where have you come from?
5 When's your birthday?
6 Can you lend me $50?
7 Who did you vote for?
8 Are you from around here?
9 Have you got a boy/girlfriend?
10 Do you believe in God?
11 What's up?
12 Did you know your flies are undone?
13 Are you being honest?
14 What did you dream about, then?
15 Can I borrow your newspaper?

© Cambridge University Press 1988

Get the students out of their seats and moving around. Ask them to compare their responses.

10.5 Stairs

The most ordinary events or objects in our experience can give rise to very meaningful language, and the more meaningful language is, the more justification there is for listening to it.

Think for a moment about steps and stairs. There may be interesting stairs in or around your present house or flat, or those of your students. Stairs were different when we were small: they were big. Maybe there have been some flights of steps you always went up or down in a certain way. Banisters and landings can be interesting. People use stairs for many things besides going up and down. Stairs can be metal, shallow, wooden, going from light into dark or the other way round.

Write a dictation passage about two or three lots of stairs that are to you in some way memorable. (Alternatively mentally prepare a passage without making notes.) Dictate the passage. Then ask the students to work in small groups and tell each other about stairs of their own.

What is happening here is that you are using the dictation as a kind of 'incubation' period during which the students are coping with your stair thoughts, but also, almost certainly beginning to have their own. They are also getting the message that you are willing to share some of your thoughts and feelings about the present and the past with them.

Think of other themes for a similar sharing of experience.

11 Community Language Learning

Earlier sections, particularly the previous one, have looked at ways of drawing on the language and personal resources of the students in developing text for dictation. It is possible to go much further in this direction by incorporating the techniques of the Silent Way and Community Language Learning and similar approaches. But this goes beyond the scope of this book.

In this section we simply offer three suggestions which take you a little further, raising some of the questions and introducing some of the techniques which Community Language Learning presents.

Our debts are apparent.

11.1 Student transcriptions (from Community Language Learning)

What is Community Language Learning?

The best answer to this question is to outline what happens in a beginners' class. The students sit in a circle with a tape recorder in the centre. You need a microphone with a longish lead and a pause button on it, or, for a smallish group, a pocket dictaphone which can be passed round. You stay outside the circle, behind the students' backs.

The conversations

When a student wants to say something to another member of the learning group she calls the teacher over and produces her utterance in the mother tongue (or the working language of the group). You whisper a translation in the target language in her ear. The student takes the mike and starts the recorder before saying what she wants to say in the target language to her addressee in the group. She then stops the machine. Her target language utterance has been recorded on the machine.

If the phrase the student wants translating is a long one, or if it requires a long translation in the target language, the teacher can segment the translation and have the student record it piece by piece. As time goes by, students usually come to realise that the production of over-long utterances for translation into the target language hinders learning.

If the addressee decides to answer she calls the teacher over and the process outlined above is repeated. But of course the addressee may decide not to reply if she has nothing to say, or if another group member gets in first with another utterance directed at someone else.

The learners have complete control of the turn-taking in the conversation and the teacher has to abandon all attempts and temptations to control what goes on. In physical terms this means that you must avoid any eye contact with the addressee of a target language utterance, as a look from the teacher could well be taken as an invitation/command to reply. You are not the group's animator in the normal meaning of this term – you become a sort of waiter hanging back in a relaxed way until called. You are ready and available, but neither propose, suggest nor impose. This is clearly a very different state of mind from the usual teacher mind-set.

Charles Curran, the originator of the approach, describes the teacher as a counsellor or informant. The precise term he uses is 'knower', in the sense of being an expert in the target language. In addition, the teacher has to be capable of consecutive translation of as many idiolects as there are learners in the group. It is vital that each learner should perceive the translations offered to her as corresponding to the mood and feel of the original utterances. Once a group gets into the swing of things, you have to try and keep up with the pace demanded of you. Even with beginners this means that you must be very fluent in both languages.

Curran's term 'counsellor' refers to the teacher's role in first recognising and then accepting and assuaging the natural anxiety that many students feel when faced with a foreign language. If the teacher notices that a student who has requested a translation is tense, she may if appropriate put a hand on the student's shoulder as she whispers the translation into his ear. This is a way of accepting, absorbing and reducing the anxiety.

The conversation part of the task will normally last 15 to 25 minutes. If it lasts longer the transcription of the utterances becomes too long and the corpus to be dealt with too heavy and thus discouraging.

Translation back into the mother tongue

Providing the students have been careful to turn the recorder on and off at the right times, everything said in the target language will be on the tape. A member of the group winds back and plays the tape, utterance by utterance, leaving time for each person to translate what she has said back into the mother tongue. It sometimes happens that a learner doesn't recognise something that she has said, or has forgotten the meaning. There is nearly always someone in the group who does remember. If nobody can remember, they will normally ask the knower. During the translation back phase, the knower is busy noting down the sentences needed for the third phase.

Language thinking

The teacher as informant writes up on the board sentences from the tape that present grammatical/visual similarities of the sort the students are likely to notice easily, and which may provoke them to ask questions. With real beginners three or four phrases may well be enough.

It is during this third phase that the knower is most likely to fall back into the trap of being a teacher and taking over the activity. To avoid this the informant tells the students that she is there to answer any questions they themselves may have about the sentences that are up on the board – their meaning, grammar, sounds, spellings or anything else the students may want to ask. This question and answer work takes place in the learners' mother tongue or in the working language of the group. It is vital that the informant does not stray beyond the role of informant and confines herself to answering only questions that have been asked.

These three stages outlined above normally constitute a lesson.

Work on the transcript

Prior to the next session, the knower transcribes the tape. The rendering must be as faithful as possible to what the students have actually said on the tape. If, in an early session, a student has really made a hash of an utterance, you should either omit it completely or transcribe a correct version. Usually, from the second session on, some learners will try out words and phrases on their own, without calling for translation, though their sentences will sometimes teem with errors.

At the start of the session the transcriptions are given out and the learners read the first page of their own group textbook. During this reading work students ask each other and ask the knower a large number of questions, as they have often forgotten two-thirds of what they discovered in the first session. The teacher must be available and helpful, but must *not* intervene, propose or test.

The work on the transcript naturally leads on to the recording of a new conversation, but this time some learners may well want to try out things they have learnt from the first dialogue.

Seems simple

The mechanics of Community Language Learning are quite simple. Session by session the group creates the next pages of their own unique textbook. The problem lies with the way the group develops. The teacher does not impose a learning style and this means that the individual learning processes of the people in the group are allowed to surface. The result is often an arduous negotiation as to how lessons should be organised, with leadership struggles and attempted hijackings. People expect learning styles to be imposed on them, and sudden freedom can feel both distressing and problematic.

11.2 Community Language Learning for larger classes

Making the tape

Split your students up into smallish groups, say a maximum of eight in each group, and arrange each group round a small tape recorder with a blank tape. Make sure you have an even number of groups. The more mobile the tape recorder the better. Ask them to record a five-minute conversation of their own (i.e. five minutes speaking time on the tape). Resist the temptation (and, usually, requests) to provide them with a topic. Explain that the conversation must be kept short as another group is going to transcribe it. Ask them to make sure everyone in the group has a say. Sit back and don't intervene unless asked. It will obviously take them longer than the time of the tape, allowing for initial discussion and pregnant pauses.

Transcribing the tapes

Now that the students have finished their tapes swap them over and ask them to transcribe one another's on to OHP transparency or paper, and to underline any errors. Have a secretary and a disc jockey for each group. If the students have been made aware that they are making the tape for another group there will often be references or messages to the members of the other group, which increase the commitment of the transcribing group.

Feedback

If the students have now finished transcribing onto an OHP transparency then bring the whole class together to correct any errors. Let the transcribing group say why they have underlined parts of the script and let the recording group try to correct with the help of the transcribing group if necessary. You might like to intervene as a last resort if an error has been missed by both groups, or to help with register. Repeat with other transcripts.

If the students have transcribed onto paper via a secretary, then rush photocopy enough copies for each student to be able to see or have a copy of each transcript. The students can then correct errors in groups, or, if they prefer, individually. You may like to go through the transcripts with the whole class at the end when most students have finished.

This variation reduces the workload for the teacher and allows her to quietly observe the students at work, i.e. the students transcribe, not the teacher. The session outlined above leaves the teacher out of the recording stage. At any level from post-beginner on the students are capable of making their own decisions about language. The teacher is more likely to be an inhibiting factor. If this activity is repeated throughout a course, the students become expert and very quick at making tapes, transcribing and correcting. To facilitate this it is important at the beginning of each recording session to ask the students how they feel about the last session and how to improve the forthcoming session. It is also useful to initiate a debriefing after the recording. Students often like to hear their tapes again during the error-correction stage and this facilitates pronunciation work. When you come to the end of a course, offer the students the chance to relisten to tapes made at the beginning. This is an excellent way of allowing students to realise what they have learnt.

More advanced groups may feel restricted by making short tapes. Let them make more extensive tapes and instead of transcribing the whole tape ask them to select five segments of 'good' English and five of 'bad' English.

11.3　Shadow Community Language Learning

Divide the class into an even number of groups of not more than ten each.

Supposing you have two groups; arrange them in concentric circles around a tape recorder. Ask the inner group to make a short tape – see the introduction to Community Language Learning on page 106. Ask the outer group to 'shadow' the inner group, giving their best attention to what the students have to say. Explain to the outer group that when the recording is finished they'll be asked to recreate the inner group's conversation as faithfully as possible.

Ask the inner and outer groups to swap places. The new inner group makes a recording of what they can remember of the previous conversation. The outer group watches and listens.

After the recordings have been made, the students transcribe the two conversations side by side on the board. They correct and discuss them.

Acknowledgement

We learnt this idea from Vincent Broderick of the International Buddhist University at Osaka, Japan.

12   Working with teachers

This book as a gift to initial trainees

When initial trainees first face a class it is a well-known fact that they often fall back on the well-tried techniques they experienced in the past as learners. Dictation comes into this category. By working in this area the trainer is accepting the reality of the trainees's previous learning experience and building on from there. This book serves as a bridge from traditional learner experience to exciting new way of teaching.

Several of our trainer colleagues have recommended the book in its Pilgrims Pilot format to their trainees at the end of one week introductory courses to TEFL and at the end of the RSA Preparatory Course. Maybe you would like to do the same?

If you want to introduce people to some of the ideas in this book, you could start by giving them this dictation:

Some of you may remember dictation from your schooldays with pleasure, to some it may have felt boring, while some may have found it an encouraging exercise. In many cases the teacher probably read you the passage, dictated it and then read it a third time so you could check through. To many people this, and nothing else, *is* dictation.

The picture begins to change if you ask yourself a series of questions:
Who gives the dictation and to who?
Who controls the pace of the dictation?
Who creates or chooses the text?
Who corrects?

If all power remains in the hands of the teacher, then we have a bleak, traditional landscape. But dictation can be otherwise ...

After your colleagues/trainees have taken down the dictation, invite them to decide what answers they can find to the questions. This should lead naturally into experiencing some of the techniques in this book.

In this exercise the trainees are *doing* what they are being asked to think about. The one 'loops' into the other like an Escher drawing. We learnt this teacher training technique from Tessa Woodward, who has applied it to many areas of methodology. When she wants to show trainees jigsaw reading for example, she gives them a jigsaw reading about jigsaw reading.

Note

An interesting book covering this area is *Goedel, Escher, Bach (An eternal golden braid)*, by D.R. Hofstadter. *Loop-Input* by Tessa Woodward shows how this idea is used in teacher training.

12.1 Transcribing teaching practice

This technique saves you, the trainer, from being *physically present* at the session that will be worked on. Perhaps less travelling? And your absence from the session could be a big plus in terms of reducing the trainee's anxiety.

Ask the trainee to take a discussion mike and a good recorder into the lesson to be 'observed'. She should place the mike so that it picks up as many student voices as possible.

She tapes X number of minutes of the lesson.

In the quiet of your own room you then get two recorders and play her lesson cassette on one, while re-recording it onto machine two. When you have a comment to make you stop machine one and record what you have to say onto machine two. Then restart machine one . . .

You hand the trainee the cassette with her lesson interspersed with your comments. She produces a transcript of this tape, writing in two columns: her lesson script on one side and your comments on the other. The purpose of this lengthy task is to let her pay really detailed attention to *her own* interaction with her students.

Acknowledgement

This transcription idea is borrowed from the training of counsellors and is described in some detail in Chapter 6 of *Counselling Techniques that Work* by W.W. Dyer and John Vriend.

12.2 Using the computer

Dictation is a useful area for self-study and the micro-computer, as has already been noted, is an excellent 'corrector' of dictations.

Describe this situation to your trainee:

The student is given an audio cassette with the spoken text of a dictation passage on it. The micro has the same text in its memory and is programmed to help the student with any mistakes she makes.

The student switches on the recorder and listens to the whole passage. She then listens to the first sentence again and types what she can of it into the computer. The computer reacts, or doesn't, if there is a mistake.

Working with teachers

Now give out a photocopy of the text below for group discussion.

Suppose you have a tame programmer sitting opposite you whose job it is to program the micro for dictation correction. You have to give her the pedagogical information which allows her to write the right kind of program. She might ask these questions:

When should the machine react to a mistake? The moment a wrong letter is typed in; at the end of the word in which there is a mistake; at the first full stop; at the end of the passage?

How should the machine react? By writing the word correctly in a box at the top of the screen; by flashing a question mark over the wrong letters; by writing the sentence at the top of the screen with the type of error identified, e.g. word, segmentation, punctuation, spacing, spelling, etc.?

How should the machine react to mistakes from a sensory point of view? Jumping letters; burglar alarms; sound effects; music; colour?

Could the machine's feedback, once the student has typed the whole passage in, be simply to show the student her own text interlined with the correct text?

Should a variety of correction modes be programmed in and the decision as to which one to choose left to the user? If so, you would need an initial menu screen. How would you succinctly describe each correction mode?

Note

Some of the facilities outlined above are available in *Microtext*, a frame-based text presentation language that runs on the BBC micro-computer. *Microtext* can be used to control a suitable audio tape recorder.

Acknowledgement

The ideas came out of a discussion we had with John Morgan, co-author of *Once Upon a Time*, and *Vocabulary*.

Answers

The answers below are the obvious answers. Students will come up with other answers, and some of these can be more unusual than the ones given here. For example in 3.1, 'Taking a message', answers have included:

> The surgeon is a priest.
> The driver was the boy's mother's first husband, the surgeon being her current husband.

1.2 'Saying it right': Peter was thanked and given a big present for saving the boss's life. He was sacked for being asleep at work.

1.6 'Word fields': Sports words are *Corner, foul, goal, start, drop, whistle, jumped, shot, let in, defensive, wall, move,* and *block.* Less obvious words that the students could make a plausible case for include *spat, interruptions,* and *row.*

3.1 'Taking a message': The obvious answer is that the surgeon is the boy's mother.

4.4 'Sounds American': a typical English name, M.A., New York, holiday, got, nice, flat, tube/underground, haven't, met, (comprehensive) school, friends, American, opposite/on the other side of the corridor, made, seeing, play, typical English name.

6.5 'Picture dictation': The quickest way for a typical person to reach the swimmer is to run to point A and to swim from there. One student said, 'It's different for a turtle.'

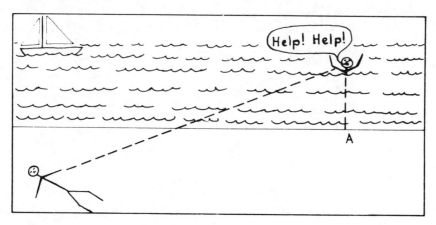

Answers

6.6 'Time dictation':
superstar, motel American English
eat, drink, speak Anglo-Saxon
veal, beef, mutton Norman
cow, sheep Anglo-Saxon
want, dirt, egg, die Viking
education, encyclopaedia, expensive Renaissance
church, angel, priest Christianity
splif, punk, new wave Punk

n.b., agenda, per annum, per capita Renaissance
man, wife, meat, house Anglo-Saxon
polaroid, blitz, ersatz American English
give, get, sister, sky Viking
demand, amorous, commence Norman
ladies' room, senior citizen, memorial park American English
crime, park, tax Norman
candle, master, school Christianity
dungarees, bangle, yoga Imperialism
adolescence, royal, sumptuous Norman
sleep, dream, weep Anglo-Saxon

7.1 'Whistle gaps': I'm walking *along* this street in Leicester you see, late one afternoon and *it's* raining, and suddenly there's this middle-*aged* woman blocking my *way*, standing in front *of* me right in the *middle* of the pavement. And she looks at me with her *eyes* glaring, and she *says*: 'Why don't all you *black* bastards go home? You come here and you take all the *jobs* and all the houses, and all you *do's* live on the Social. You've none of you ever done a *decent* day's work in your lives. So go on, clear *out*, go back to the *jungle* where you came from!'

9.2 'The messenger and the scribe': The judge knows that the doughnut seller's coin will be oily. Oil will float to the top when that coin is put into the water.

9.4 'The never-ending story': $20, assuming that the value of the shoes to the shop assistant is $12.

Bibliography

Bandler, Richard and Grinder, John, *The Structure of Magic* vols. I and II, Science and Behaviour Books, Inc., 1976.

Bandler, Richard and Grinder, John, *Tranceformations: Neuro-Linguistic Programming*, Real People Press, 1981.

Bandler, Richard and Grinder, John, *Frogs into Princes*, Real People Press, 1981.

Baudain, Richard and Marjorie, *Oggi che Facciamo*, Pilgrims Publications, 1986.

Bliss, Alan, *A Dictionary of Foreign Words and Phrases*, Routledge & Kegan Paul, 1966.

Changeux, Jean-Pierre, *Neuronal Man*, Pantheon Books, 1985.

Cleveland, Bernard, *Master Teaching Techniques*, Connecting Link Press, 1984.

Cormican, John and Stanford, Gene, *A Guidebook for Teaching about the English Language*, Allyn & Bacon, 1979.

Curran, Charles, *Counselling Learning: A whole person model for education*, Apple River Press, 1972.

Dufeu, Bernard, 'La psychodramaturgie linguistique', *Le Français dans le Monde*, February/March, 1983.

Dyer, W. W. and Vriend, J., *Counselling Techniques that Work*, APGA Press, 1975.

Ely, Philip, *Bring the Lab Back to Life*, Pergamon, 1984.

Frank, Christine and Rinvolucri, Mario, *Challenge to Think*, Oxford University Press, 1982.

Frank, Christine and Rinvolucri, Mario, *Grammar in Action*, Pergamon, 1983.

Gattegno, Caleb, *Teaching Foreign Languages in Schools the Silent Way*, Educational Solutions, 1972.

Gattegno, Caleb, *The Common Sense of Teaching Foreign Languages*, Educational Solutions, 1976.

Hofstadter, D. R., *Goedel, Escher, Bach (An eternal golden braid)*, Penguin, 1979.

Jaoui, Gysa and Gourdin, Claude, *Transactions*, Inter Editions, 1982. (in French)

Maley, Alan and Grellet, Françoise, *Mind Matters*, Cambridge University Press, 1981.

McArthur, Tom, *Longman Lexicon of Contemporary English*, Longman, 1981.

Morgan, John and Rinvolucri, Mario, *Once Upon a Time*, Cambridge University Press, 1983.

Morgan, John and Rinvolucri, Mario, *The Q Book*, Longman 1988.

Bibliography

Morgan, John and Rinvolucri, Mario, *Vocabulary*, Oxford University Press, 1986.

Pfeiffer, J. W. and Jones, J. E. (editors), *A Handbook of Structured Experiences for Human Relations Training*, University Associates, 1974.

Spaven*a, Lou (editor), *Towards the Creative Teaching of English*, Heinemann Educational Books, 1980.

Stevenson, Victor (editor), *Words*, Macdonald, 1983.

Stevick, Earl, *Memory, Meaning and Method*, Newbury House, 1976.

Stevick, Earl, *A Way and Ways*, Newbury House, 1980.

Swan, Michael and Walter, Catherine, *The Cambridge English Course 2*, Cambridge University Press, 1984.

Syer, John and Connolly, Christopher, *Sporting Body, Sporting Mind: an athlete's guide to mental training*, Cambridge University Press, 1984.

Tomscha, Terry, *Practical English Teaching*, III, 4, June, 1983.

Woodward, Tessa, *Loop-Input*, Pilgrims Publications, 1988.

Index

It is hoped that this index will provide a way into the book for teachers by providing an indication of where to find topics, language and methods which will fit in with their thinking and planning.

Index

Index of levels

This index groups the different exercises according to the level of the sample text in this book.

3.1 Taking a message
3.4 Seeking information
3.5 Instant lesson
4.4 Sounds American
5.4 Quantifying sentences
6.5 Picture dictation
7.2 Words → dictation → story
7.5 Piecing it together
7.7 Mutual dictation
8.1 Adjectives
8.3 Before and after
8.4 What have I done?
9.2 The messenger and the scribe
9.4 The never-ending story
9.7 Musical script
10.1 The teacher's autobiography
10.2 About myself
10.3 How can you say that?
10.4 Who can you say what to?

1.1 Speed control
4.1 Connections
4.2 Collocations
4.5 The senses
5.2 Does it mean anything?
6.1 Words on a picture
6.2 Import/export
6.4 Around and about
7.1 Whistle gaps
8.6 Half the story

1.6 Word fields
4.3 Words change
5.1 Associations

4.6 Word sets
5.3 Translating ambiguity
6.6 Time dictation
7.3 Cheating dictation
9.6 Visualisation

7.6 Dictogloss

Dictation objected to

Dictation objected to: a nineteenth-century commentator's view.

The following is taken from Claude Marcel's *Language as a Means of Mental Culture and International Communication*, Vol. II, published by Chapman and Hall, London, 1853.

Dictation, so generally resorted to, is inefficient as an orthographical exercise. In Italian and Spanish, the conformity of the orthography with the pronunciation renders it utterly useless. So uniform is the power of the letters in these languages, that to pronounce an Italian or a Spanish word is to spell it. In German, dictation is not much more useful, because the same letters, usually representing the same sounds and articulations, it suffices to know the power of their alphabetical characters to deduce the spelling of the words from their sounds. In French, it may assist in teaching the orthography, provided the learner is made acquainted with the principles of orthoëpy and etymology, as also with the rules of grammatical concord which govern the inflection of words. But this part of the English language can never be taught through dictation, either to natives or foreigners. He who knows the spelling of an English word derives no benefit from writing it, and he who is not previously acquainted with it, will seldom be able to spell it from hearing.

In any language in which the orthography does not exactly correspond to the pronunciation, dictation is inefficient, since the writer has, thereby, no clue by which he can infer the mode of writing it from the manner in which it is uttered. This exercise, however, can be very useful as a test by which to ascertain the pupil's progress in spelling; for, although it cannot prevent the commission of errors, it affords the means of detecting and correcting them. But, viewed even in this light, dictation should not be practised frequently; because, for one word that the child may, by this means, learn to spell, he wastes time in writing a great many which he knew before. This is purchasing too dearly a species of information which can be easily acquired conjointly with higher departments of composition. Dictation is so universally resorted to, only because it gives little trouble to the instructor and demands on his part neither talent nor information.

Acknowledgement

Thanks to Tony Howatt for providing this extract.